The post–World War II paradigm that ensured security and prosperity for the Japanese people has lost much of its effectiveness. The current generation has become increasingly resentful of Japan's prolonged economic stagnation and feels a sense of drift and uncertainty about the future of the country's foreign policy.

In *Japanese Foreign Policy at the Crossroads*, Yutaka Kawashima clarifies some of the defining parameters of Japan's foreign policy and examines the challenges it currently faces, including the quagmire on the Korean Peninsula, the future of the U.S.-Japan alliance, the management of Japan-China relations, and Japan's relations with Southeast Asia.

Kawashima—who, as vice minister of foreign affairs, was Japan's highest-ranking foreign service official—cautions Japan against attempts to ensure its security and well-being outside of an international framework. He believes it crucial that Japan work with as many like-minded countries as possible to construct a regional and international order based on shared interests and shared values. In an era of globalization, he cautions, such efforts will be crucial to maintaining global world order and ensuring civilized interaction among all states.

Japanese Foreign
Policy at the Crossroads

JAPANESE FOREIGN POLICY AT THE CROSSROADS

Challenges and Options for the Twenty-First Century

YUTAKA KAWASHIMA

BROOKINGS INSTITUTION PRESS
Washington, D.C.

Copyright © 2003
THE BROOKINGS INSTITUTION
1775 Massachusetts Avenue, N.W., Washington, D.C. 20036
www.brookings.edu

Library of Congress Cataloging-in-Publication data

Kawashima, Yutaka, 1942–
    Japanese foreign policy at the crossroads / Yutaka Kawashima.
        p. cm.
    Includes bibliographical references and index.
    ISBN 0-8157-4870-1 (cloth : alk. paper)
    1. Japan—Foreign relations—1989– I. Title.
    DS891.2.K39 2003
    327.52—dc22   2003016802

9 8 7 6 5 4 3 2 1

The paper used in this publication meets minimum requirements of the American National Standard for Information Sciences—Permanence of Paper for Printed Library Materials: ANSI Z39.48-1992.

Typeset in Sabon

Composition by Cynthia Stock
Silver Spring, Maryland

Printed by R. R. Donnelley
Harrisonburg, Virginia

Contents

Preface   vii

1   *Historical Parameters of Japanese Foreign Policy*   1

2   *Security Ties between Japan and the United States*   22

3   *The Economic Relationship between Japan and the United States*   55

4   *Endgame on the Korean Peninsula*   73

5   *Relations between Japan and China*   95

6   *Japan's Southeast Asia Policy*   110

7   *Japan's Relations with Europe*   126

8   *Striving for Peace and Saving Failed States*   135

Bibliography   153

Index   155

Preface

It has been an entirely new experience for me to write a book. Although I drafted numerous cables and policy papers during the thirty-seven years that I worked in the Japanese Foreign Ministry, much of what I wrote pertained to confidential diplomatic matters and few people had access to it. I never imagined that one day I might be tempted to produce a book for the general public. However, in 2002, while teaching a course, "Decisionmaking in Japanese Foreign Policy," jointly with Ezra Vogel at the Kennedy School of Government at Harvard University, I was shocked to find that the supply of material in English covering the evolution of Japan's foreign policy since the end of the cold war was very meager. The paucity may be due to the fact that the era is still too fresh to pique the appetite of historians. Perhaps a more likely explanation is that as Japan's economy lost much of its dynamism and no longer was perceived as a threat, curiosity on the part of Americans and other foreigners about the "inscrutable" Japanese started to wane. In any case, I began to think that it would be worthwhile to produce a book analyzing the evolution of Japan's foreign policy in the postwar era, with emphasis on the period since 1990.

I was fascinated by reading *Special Providence: American Foreign Policy and How It Changed the World*, by Walter Russell Mead, in which he presents four basic ways of looking at American foreign policy: the Hamiltonian, Wilsonian, Jeffersonian, and Jacksonian approaches. Although we do not have their exact counterparts in Japan, I decided to emulate his book by clarifying various schools of thought that have constituted decisive parameters of Japanese foreign policy. For example, the interaction—or rather, the confrontation—between realists and pacifists has dominated decisionmaking on the issue of national security. The debate over maintaining a distinctly "Asian identity" or attempting to "catch up with the West" also has often had a defining impact on Japan's foreign policy agenda. Over the years from 1974 to 1995, working alternately in the American Affairs Bureau and the Asian Affairs Bureau and also at the Japanese embassies in Washington and Seoul, I became keenly aware of this dichotomy, which has been one of the key parameters of Japan's foreign policy.

As any diplomat should be, I have been keenly interested in security issues. I was fortunate in having been posted in three countries in which the defining wars of the second half of the twentieth century—the Korean War, the Vietnam War, and the series of wars in the Middle East—were fought. I served in Saigon, South Vietnam, from 1969 to 1971, which was one year after the Tet offensive; in Seoul, Republic of Korea, from 1992 to 1993, during the time that tension over North Korea's development of nuclear weapons accelerated; and in Tel Aviv, Israel, from 1997 to 1999, when the peace process under the Oslo Accord was still being pursued. For these three countries, survival had been at the absolute top of the agenda since their founding, and South Vietnam eventually failed in that regard. In particular, I was very much impressed with the unshakable legitimacy accorded to the armed forces in Israel, which were regarded as the ultimate guarantor of the survival of the state. That constituted a stark contrast with the attitude in Japan, where many people hesitated to accept the legitimacy of the Japanese Self-Defense Force because of the historical memory of the fanatical Imperial military forces, which led the country to devastating defeat in World War II. My impression is that it took almost half a century for the Japanese people to accept the legitimacy of the Self-Defense Force, which has proved to be devoted to the defense of Japan, operating under full democratic control and within constitutional constraints, and in that sense totally different from its predecessor. Since the end of World War II, Japan, unlike the three countries mentioned, has been extremely fortunate in not having had to face a crisis that could threaten its very survival.

Regarding the pursuit of prosperity, I joined the Foreign Ministry in the mid-1960s, when we were obsessed with our vulnerable foreign exchange reserves of only U.S.$2 billion. Those were the days when Japan was about to graduate from the class of developing countries to the class of advanced economies, starting on a path of robust economic development marked by a double-digit growth rate every year. I belong, therefore, to the generation that witnessed the respect and eventually the fear that Japan evoked in the international community for the dynamism and increasing competitiveness of its economy. Today, the time around the 1980s when Japan was considered a serious economic threat to the United States and the West European countries seems like a remote, bygone era.

My basic premise in this book is that the sharing of interests and values among nations has become a basic and perhaps an irreversible trend in today's world. This creates a setting that is totally different from what my generation was trained to face during the cold war. It is my strong belief that in order for Japan to meet the challenges discussed in this book, it must work with as many like-minded countries as possible to enhance the effectiveness of the international order, deepening and widening the shared interests and values on which that order is based. Firm in that conviction, I revisit some past foreign policy decisions that brought success in the quest for peace and prosperity and examine the evolution of a new foreign policy posture in the aftermath of the cold war. I conclude by speculating on new challenges that Japan might encounter in the coming years.

In closing, I wish to say that this book represents my personal views alone; it does not in any way reflect the position of the Japanese government.

YUTAKA KAWASHIMA
Tokyo
June 2003

Acknowledgments

At the outset, I wish to say that I am deeply indebted to Mike Armacost, former president of the Brookings Institution, and to Jim Steinberg, vice president and director of Foreign Policy Studies at Brookings. As a senior officer in the Ministry of Foreign Affairs, I had worked with both of them on many important occasions in the past when they occupied various key posts in the U.S. government. Soon after my retirement from the ministry, they kindly invited me to Brookings as a distinguished visiting scholar in the fall of 2001. My time within the institution's intellectually stimulating environment presented a truly invaluable opportunity to reflect on the basic orientation of Japan's foreign policy. I should stress also that without the help of Ezra Vogel, this book would have been nonexistent. Ezra invited me to teach a course on decisionmaking in Japanese foreign policy at the Kennedy School of Government in 2002. It was primarily the wonderful experience of teaching that course that prompted me to write this book, and I am very much indebted to the brilliant students who made so many inspiring comments during our classes. I also owe much to Makoto Iokibe of Kobe University and Bunji Abe of the

Osaka University of Education, who gave me valuable advice while they were doing research at Harvard in 2002.

Naturally, I am profoundly indebted to the numerous wonderful colleagues with whom I worked in the Japanese Foreign Ministry—many more than I can name here. This book is, after all, the distilled version of what I learned from them over the thirty-seven years of my career in the ministry.

Finally I wish to express my gratitude to Eileen Hughes, who edited my manuscript with superb professionalism, and to the other members of the Brookings Institution Press who did such a wonderful job in producing this book: Tanjam Jacobson, copy editor; Janet Walker, managing editor; Larry Converse, production manager; Susan Woollen, art coordinator; and Becky Clark, marketing director. The whole publication process was entirely new to me, and I thoroughly enjoyed it.

1 | Historical Parameters of Japanese Foreign Policy

The basic objective of the foreign policy of Japan, like that of any other country, is to ensure the nation's security and prosperity. It can be concluded that Japan has succeeded in the pursuit of that objective for more than half a century. Since the end of World War II, Japan somehow has managed to ensure that the wars, revolutions, and other crises witnessed in East Asia throughout the period have not fatally damaged its own security. And Japan has benefited immensely from the international economic order imposed by the Bretton Woods system, without which its economic recovery and ensuing economic success would not have been possible.

Today, however, a sense of drift or uncertainty about the future course of foreign policy seems to prevail in Japan. In part, it reflects uncertainty about the international situation. More than a decade has passed since the end of the cold war, during which international affairs were much more predictable. And yet a clear-cut concept for a new international order in the twenty-first century has yet to emerge. Many Japanese, although they may fully support the U.S. antiterrorism campaign, have begun to wonder how President George W. Bush's preemptive strike doctrine will affect the U.S.-Japanese alliance in the future. The stunning admission by North Korea of its abduction of numbers of innocent Japanese in the 1970s and 1980s and the announcement of its decision to restart its nuclear facilities have reminded the Japanese people of the urgent need to rethink how best to deal with the dangerous quagmire in the Korean Peninsula. Furthermore, as the Japanese watch the dynamic economic growth of China—in such contrast to the economic stagnation in Japan—many naturally wonder what East Asia will look like, say, twenty years from now.

Since today change is occurring everywhere at a truly exponential rate, some sense of uncertainty may be inevitable. Still, the main reasons for the sense of uncertainty evident in Japan today are indigenous. First, there is generational turnover. All the decisions that have defined the course of Japan's foreign policy were made long ago. With the passing of time, the heated debates and agonized decisionmaking of former political leaders are forgotten. Although today's younger generation is aware in an abstract sense of the importance of U.S.-Japanese relations, it seems to have difficulty grasping in any real sense the enormous stakes that Japan has in managing those relations. The domestic political tension that the leaders of the Liberal Democratic Party (LDP) had to deal with in opting to maintain security ties with the United States has become a dim memory of a bygone era. Today, the argument that the relationship between Japan and the United States is the cornerstone of Japan's foreign policy may sound like nothing but a cliché to many people. For that matter, in the 1970s and 1980s maintaining a friendly relationship with China was recognized as extremely important, and it evoked a certain sense of achievement among many Japanese who remembered the historical context and the difficulties that the two countries had to overcome to develop that relationship. But today, to a younger generation that does not share the memory, arguments of the importance of the friendship between Japan and China are hardly convincing. Moreover, today important policy statements, domestic and foreign, tend to be presented as "sound bites," and the complexity of the issues involved can easily be overlooked.

Second, in spite of the new culture of transparency and accountability in politics, the public seldom has access to the candid, in-depth analysis conducted by national decisionmakers of other countries' intentions, motives, and domestic power structure. Although such analysis is a prerequisite for successful decisionmaking, if countries began to disclose their assessments of each other publicly, the resolution of issues and problems would become much more complicated, and mutually embarrassing outcomes inevitable. Candid and even unkind assessments of adversaries may be made public if officials do not care about further negative impact on relations that already are in bad shape. However, with the end of the cold war, such cases of openly adversarial relations between countries have become rare.

Much of the art of diplomacy lies in nations' ability to assess and analyze one another continually and accurately. If the analysis or assessment shatters the conventional wisdom, it may be welcome. The process, however, cannot be made transparent. That constraint may be very frustrating for the general public. In the course of discussions among members of the so-called Committee to Change the Foreign Ministry, it was argued that the ministry should make public all analyses and conclusions regarding policy alternatives before making any foreign policy decisions. The growing demand for such transparency is bound to make it an increasingly daunting task for the government to obtain better understanding and broader support among the population for its foreign policy.

Finally, we are witnessing a crisis of legitimacy. The prolonged economic difficulties in Japan have gradually taken a toll on Japan's national psyche. The domestic mood has become more resentful. The public harbors animosity toward various things—the bureaucracy, the banking sector, the traditional political process, foreign countries. In the face of protracted difficulty, people tend to react in one of two ways: one is to reflect on what they themselves did wrong; the other is to find someone or something else to blame. The latter reaction may be seen in the actions of Islamic fundamentalist-terrorists, but it is common throughout the world. Another example is the anti-immigration fervor in various European countries, where some nationals blame foreign workers for all sorts of problems. In Japan, one gets the impression that the public has become much more supportive of a tough, hawkish, assertive, and occasionally confrontational posture in the conduct of foreign policy. Since the mid-1990s, domestic criticism of the Foreign Ministry for being subservient to the United States, subservient to China, and soft on South Korea, North Korea, and many other countries has tended to be far more frequent.

Furthermore, a series of scandals involving fraud that have erupted in the Foreign Ministry since 2001 have badly damaged its credibility and legitimacy—so much so that there is a genuine risk that much of Japan's basic foreign policy may also lose its credibility and come to be viewed with skepticism or disdain.

Japanese Foreign Policy since World War II

This chapter revisits past decisions that have constituted the basis of Japanese foreign policy since the end of World War II. Some key decisionmaking processes of the postwar era are reviewed first, and then some reflections about future options on key issues are presented. However, before embarking on a review, it is important to have a clearer idea about the key domestic parameters—constraints, identity issues, obsessions, and other factors—related to foreign policy decisionmaking. For easier understanding, these parameters are discussed to the extent possible in a dialectical manner.

Catching Up with the West versus Maintaining an Asian Identity

Ever since Japan embarked upon modernization, many Japanese leaders have been acutely aware of a dichotomy in the national identity. A famous essay by Chomin Nakae vividly describes a hypothetical discussion between two characters in which one fervently argues that Japan should "get out of Asia" and join the club of Western powers while the other insists that Japan should remain an Asian nation. After all, the modernization effort since the Meiji Restoration can be simply defined as a nationwide attempt to catch up with the West. There were two phases of this catch-up process. The first was from the Meiji Restoration in 1868 to World War II, in which the fruit of the first phase was utterly destroyed. The second phase was from 1945 to sometime in the 1970s, when Japan became a major industrial power. When Japan was invited to the first summit of major industrial democracies (the gathering of the "G-6," as Canada was not invited to the first meeting), there was a genuine sense of achievement in Japan, where many naturally thought that membership in that kind of forum signified the successful conclusion of the catch-up process. Since then, Japan's identity as a responsible member of the major industrial democracies has become highly important, and it should be borne in mind in grappling with various foreign policy issues.

During the period from 1868 to 1945, there was not much conflict between the two approaches in terms of policy implications. To catch up with the West and perhaps to preempt any risk of colonization by Western powers, Japan vigorously participated in the game of imperialism in Asia. To "get out of Asia" was never an actual course of action. Instead, Japan's Asian identity was stressed in terms of resentment toward the hegemony of the Western powers, notably the United Kingdom until the early 1930s and the United States afterward. Fumimaro Konoe, who became prime minister in the late 1930s, published an essay in 1918 decrying the supremacy of the United Kingdom and the United States in international politics that had considerable resonance at the time among the elite class in Japan.

"Japan's Asian identity" is almost a tautology. However, since World War II various arguments in favor of specific courses of action have been advanced on the basis of that identity. And often those arguments have tended to reflect Japanese psychological reservations about—or in some cases even revulsion toward—what the West embodies. A typical case in point is the issue of values, notably human rights.

The Japanese people today are thoroughly committed to universal values such as freedom and democracy. However, whenever it appears that Westerners are eager to press their human rights agenda on Asian countries, the Japanese often claim that Asian values are different. Japan, as an Asian country, should point out those differences, the argument goes—for example, by refusing to join Western efforts to impose sanctions on certain Asian countries because of human rights violations. Moreover, the theory used to be expounded that enlightened dictatorial regimes in various East Asian countries were the key to their successful economic development. And it has been frequently argued throughout East Asia that Asians attach more importance to and emphasis on group-oriented values, such as the importance of the family, and that those values have been the key to social cohesion and success in nation building. For example, in the early 1990s Singapore's leaders often expressed the view that there was little doubt that a society with communitarian values, where the interest of society takes precedence over that of the individual, suits them better than the individualism of America. The very success of some East Asian countries in achieving dynamic economic development gave a certain degree of legitimacy to these arguments in defense of Asian values. However, treating what can be argued to be a universal value as a parochial value of the West to be contrasted with Asian values is of debatable validity. Nevertheless, when issues are discussed in the context of the differences between Western culture, values, or standards and those of Asia, the argument that, because of its Asian identity, Japan should act differently from the West can have considerable impact on popular opinion.

Another interesting case in point was the East Asian Economic Caucus (EAEC) issue in the early 1990s. Prime Minister Mahathir bin Mohamad of Malaysia proposed forming the EAEC, whose membership was supposed to include all members of the Association of Southeast Asian Nations (ASEAN), Japan, China, and the Republic of Korea (ROK). If this group had been a formal economic entity, something like a trade bloc, perhaps arguments about its pros and cons would have been clearer, because its economic advantages and disadvantages would have been easily identifiable. However, since Mahathir's proposal was to establish an informal forum with a very loosely defined agenda, the debate inside Japan centered solely on the identity question. The Asian identity school held that there was nothing wrong with the idea of East Asians getting together to talk about economic problems pertaining to East Asia and that Japan, as an Asian nation, should wholeheartedly support the scheme. The industrial democracy identity school held that the notion of excluding countries like the United States, Canada, Australia, and New Zealand could be counterproductive at a time when APEC (Asia Pacific Economic Cooperation forum) was starting to do well; besides, the United States was adamantly opposed to such a group, claiming that it would undermine APEC. In any event, the EAEC became a nonissue in the late 1990s, when a new forum for dialogue between Asia and Europe was created at the joint initiative of Singapore and France. The participants from Asia were limited to ASEAN members, Japan, China, and the ROK, and European participants were limited to European Union (EU) members. Thus a precedent was established for forming a group, the membership of which was de facto EAEC, without much agonizing about the possible impact on Pacific unity.

Pacifists versus Realists on the Security Issue

The clash between pacifists and realists regarding the peace and security of Japan has persisted since the end of World War II. In view of the catastrophic casualties that Japan had suffered during the war, it is natural that the Japanese people came to have an extremely strong aversion to war and anything related to the military. And in the immediate aftermath of the war, the foremost concern of the United States was to eliminate any possibility of the reemergence of the military in Japan. Therefore, at the initiative of the United States, a new constitution was promulgated that included a provision, Article 9, that if read literally seemed to preclude any possibility of Japan's regaining its defense capability. As described in chapter 2 of this volume, many Japanese government officials in those days assumed that in the event of an attack on Japan, the United Nations would take care of Japan's defense with its own forces, as envisioned in Chapter 7 of the UN Charter. However, the advent of the cold war at the end of the 1940s totally altered Japan's circumstances. Instead of ensuring the security of the United States against Japan, ensuring the security of Japan against the newly emerging threat from the communist bloc became the more urgent priority for the United States. In response to U.S. pressure to proceed with the rearmament of Japan, Prime Minister Shigeru Yoshida eventually opted for forming what was described as a "lightly armed mercantile state." The gist of Japan's defense policy was the establishment of security ties with the United States and the eventual creation of the relatively small Japanese Self-Defense Force (JSDF).

In the past, the domestic debate between pacifists and realists over the peace and security of Japan quite often led to fierce political turmoil. Three notable features of the debate should be pointed out. First, it often takes the form not so much of a policy argument as of legalistic scrutiny focusing primarily on the constitutional constraint on military action. Second, the crux of the debate is whether the notion of deterrence is accepted or not. Third, at issue is whether and to what extent even the democratically elected government can be trusted never to return to the path toward militarism, which had led Japan into war, with tragic consequences.

LEGALISM. In the course of parliamentary debate, the opposition parties try to attack the government by taking up the legalistic aspects of the defense issue. From the pacifist viewpoint, "rearming" Japan by creating the JSDF—as well as maintaining security ties with the United States—is an unforgivable breach of the constitution. Also, the opposition has always been a minority in the Diet, so if the debate is about the policy options related to security, the opposition is bound to be numerically overwhelmed. However, as long as the debate is about the legality of the government's action, the opposition can proclaim what the government is doing to be unconstitutional and illegal.

Moreover, the assumption is that government agencies carry out their functions exactly as they are stipulated in the authorizing laws and regulations. Therefore, for example, the law related to the role and functions of the JSDF had to be amended so that JSDF aircraft could be used to evacuate Japanese nationals in foreign countries. In any other country, it would be inconceivable that aircraft of the national defense force could not be used for such purpose unless a specific clause was included in the law.

As to the constitutional constraint on military action, the debate often is related to the definition of "use of force." The constitution permits the use of force—that is, military action by the JSDF—only for individual self-defense (to fight foreign forces that are engaged in armed attack on Japan) and not for collective self-defense (defense of allies, for example). However, things are not that simple. The legal question is always raised of whether the apparently noncombat logistical support activities of the JSDF, such as supplying materiel to U.S. forces (USF), facilitating refueling of U.S. combat aircraft and ships, and providing medical support to the USF can be considered to constitute the use of force. The government's interpretation of the constitution is that they can, as long as they are part of combat operations. An often-quoted example is that to engage the JSDF in transporting materiel to the front line, where actual combat is going on, constitutes an integral part of the use of force and therefore is unconstitutional.

This is a serious question that requires a clear-cut response. Following the enactment in 1999 of a law paving the way for logistical support activities by the JSDF for the USF in the vicinity of Japan—and in 2001 of a law defining measures to deal with terrorism in the aftermath of 9/11—the government was authorized to engage the JSDF in various non-combat support activities for the USF. However, as Prime Minister Junichiro Koizumi suggested, the opposition's legal arguments against those laws sometimes were as relevant as medieval theological debates. Thus far the issue has not been clearly sorted out. It has often been pointed out that if the standing interpretation of the constitution were revised to accept the constitutionality of the exercise of collective self-defense, then the need for elaborating on the definition of "use of force" in the context of logistical support by the JSDF for the USF would practically disappear.

Another unique aspect of the legal battle is that the government is expected to maintain the legal consistency of all the answers it has given in past parliamentary debates. If there are frequent changes of the governing parties, the new governing party can claim that it is not bound by the legal positions of the previous government. However, in Japan, because the LDP has stayed in power continuously for decades, the LDP government is required to maintain the continuity of its legal arguments. For example, in parliamentary debate about the interpretation of the security treaty between Japan and the United States, responses of government officials some forty years ago have to be quoted and adhered to.

THE NOTION OF DETERRENCE. In essence, the pacifist view is characterized by the rejection of the notion of deterrence. Maintaining deterrence by establishing security ties with the United States and forming the JSDF is viewed as a dangerous ploy that can entangle Japan in another war. This fear of entanglement had considerable resonance among the Japanese people throughout the postwar era. During the cold war era in particular, the Japanese had a strong psychological impulse to distance themselves from the prospect of the horrific devastation that could ensue if the hostility between the two sides erupted in a nuclear exchange.

It also should be noted that the implicit assumption was that as long as Japan refrained from engaging in military provocation, the risk of entanglement in warfare would be minimized, because the invasion of a harmless Japan by foreign powers was deemed unlikely. Many Japanese share the belief that the Mongolians' attempt to invade Japan in the twelfth century was the only instance of invasion by foreigners and that, with the exception of World War I, all the wars that Japan fought in the modern era were initiated by Japan. Of course, one may be tempted to call this view typical of an insular mentality. Still, the perception that unless Japan starts war, the country can avoid war and enjoy perpetual peace constitutes the basis of Japanese pacifism, inasmuch as it logically rejects the notion of deterrence. This perception is in marked contrast to the lessons of history learned by the Europeans, who harbor vivid memories of centuries of mutual invasion.

Ever since Prime Minister Yoshida opted to create a lightly armed mercantile state—a decision eventually designated the Yoshida Doctrine—the conservative Japanese polity, which can be described as "realist," has adhered to the maintenance of effective deterrence for the security of Japan in spite of persistent opposition by pacifists. Whenever it has been necessary to take legislative action related to the maintenance of effective deterrence or to the role of the JSDF—such as the revision of the security treaty between Japan and the United States, the reversion of Okinawa to Japanese control, or more recently, peacekeeping operations (PKO) and measures related to the fight against terrorism—highly emotionally charged debate often has erupted between the LDP government and the opposition parties and some newspapers that are staunchly committed to the pacifist philosophy. However, over time public understanding and support of deterrence has become stronger. There has been a marked shift in the opinion polls in the degree of acceptance of the JSDF and the security ties between Japan and the United States. For example, according to polls conducted since the end of the 1960s, the percentage of those who favored maintenance of security ties and the JSDF was 40.9 percent in 1969, 64.6 percent in 1981, and 71.2 percent in 2000. Meanwhile the percentage of those favoring the abrogation of the security ties and the abolition of the JSDF was 9.6 percent in 1969, 7.6 percent in 1981, and 5.8 percent in 2000.

Especially since the end of the cold war, a series of new legislative actions have been taken authorizing the government to engage the JSDF in various noncombat missions abroad, such as peacekeeping missions and logistical support activities for U.S. forces. Sending the JSDF abroad was a hardcore taboo during the cold war era, and the pacifists did their utmost to block proposed legislation to expand the JSDF's role. The very fact that the government could overcome the opposition and manage to enact the laws signifies that perhaps Japan is entering a new phase in terms of the age-old clash between pacifists and realists. The changes that have affected the role and mission of the JSDF are discussed in chapter 2. Meanwhile, it seems safe to assume that a majority of the Japanese people have come to understand that—within the basic constraint that the use of force is prohibited except for individual self-defense—the role and mission of the JSDF should be redefined in order to address newly emerging security challenges in the aftermath of the cold war.

Finally, one unique feature of the pacifist-realist clash should be pointed out. In the realm of international politics, the concepts of peace and security often are used in tandem and treated as virtually synonymous. However, in the clash between pacifist and realist in Japan, that is not quite the case. The notion of peace has become the exclusive property of the pacifists. The pacifists tend to view "security" as the opposite of "peace" and therefore pejorative, in that the notion of security is likely to be used as justification for the policy of deterrence, which the pacifists detest. In essence, the "peace-loving" opposition fiercely attacks the realists, who preach the importance of the "security" of Japan.

CONFIDENCE IN JAPAN'S DEMOCRACY. After World War II, the Japanese people felt strongly that they had been badly betrayed by the imperial government, which had led Japan into war and inflicted so much damage and suffering on ordinary citizens. They became very distrustful of the government's role in anything related to peace and security, and that distrust helped the pacifists greatly in their efforts to oppose the government's security policies. For the generation whose memory of the prewar era was still fresh, claims that Japan was back on the slippery slope to war or that once again citizens would be haunted by the intrusions of the military police were entirely credible, and cries such as "We will never again allow our sons to be slaughtered in war" had considerable resonance. Because they had suffered so much as a consequence of the militarism of the prewar era, many of them tended to assume that there was an inverse relation between the strength of the military and the degree of democracy—the stronger the military, the weaker the nation's democratic values. That attitude is in marked contrast with that in many other democratic countries, such as the United States, where the country's military generally is perceived to be the guarantor of the democratic values that its citizens cherish. The clash between pacifist and realist could be boiled down to one question: If a democratically elected government is responsible for all decisions pertaining to national security, is the democracy so fragile that it will be jeopardized if the nation is able to defend itself? That is precisely the question that *Yomiuri*, the newspaper with the largest circulation in Japan, raised in the mid-1980s in support of the assertive posture that Prime Minister Yasuhiro Nakasone had taken on various defense issues. *Yomiuri* argued that almost four decades after the end of World War II, democracy in Japan was strong enough to dispel any possibility of the resurgence of militarism.

Clearly the clash between pacifists and realists and the difference in their perceptions regarding the relationship between defense and democracy is the product of their different historical memories. Things therefore cannot be settled simply by logical argument. Again, over time the significance that new generations attach to these issues will gradually change; still, these themes are bound to recur whenever Japan faces a new security agenda.

Realpolitik versus the Idealistic Approach

The classic conflict between fundamental human values and the national interest—or idealism and realism—in the conduct of diplomacy has been amply discussed in many books on foreign policy. It certainly has affected Japan's foreign policy as well. One often wonders whether the argument that a policy serves Japan's national interest or the argument that it is Japan's moral obligation has more appeal and therefore a better chance of gaining the support of the general public. In many cases, the principle of respecting human values and the principle of serving the national interest are not starkly different in their application. In late 1980s, the Japanese government presented the concept of contributing to the maintenance of international order as the cornerstone of Japan's foreign policy. The idea was that in this way Japan would help to ensure the peace and prosperity of all mankind. Obviously such a policy orientation can be justified by either argument.

Still, there have been many instances in which Japan has had to agonize over the issue. But before proceeding to the discussion of those cases, some clarification is needed of the concepts of "national interest" and "human values" in Japan's foreign policy. When people talk about the pursuit of the national interest in the context of realpolitik, they commonly think of the maneuvers to maintain the balance of power in nineteenth-century Europe. Various arguments have been presented for applying the European model to Asia, bringing about an Asian balance of power by weaving a network of alliances, ententes, or so-called strategic relationships among major players, including the United States. Particularly notable is the emergence of a new school of thought in Japan that stresses the importance to Japan of having better relations with India or Russia as a counterforce to China. That strategy certainly is a product of the end of the cold war, and it reflects the sense of uncertainty and anxiety among the Japanese about China's future course, given the country's sheer size and robust economic growth, as well as the fact that a considerable portion of the fruit of that growth is allocated for defense.

During the cold war era, the rapprochement between the United States and China brought about by Henry Kissinger in 1971 was certainly a classical success of the realpolitik approach. However, from the standpoint of the realist school in Japan in those days, Asia was not yet prepared for the balance of power game, simply because the cold war persisted and the crucial issue was the conflict between the United States and the Soviet Union. The major concern of the realists in Japan was the maintenance of a credible alliance with the United States, as well as of the effective defense capability of the JSDF. As far as the domestic debate was concerned, it was not for the most part between realists and idealists, but between realists and pacifists. But because the pacifists monopolized the ideal of peace, the debate gave the impression of being a clash between realists and idealists.

Human values were not treated as the key parameter of Japan's foreign policy in the cold war era for a number of reasons. Today, there is virtual consensus in Japan that the communist regimes were undemocratic, dictatorial, and therefore, in terms of the basic principles of democracy and freedom, failed systems. However, during the early phase of the cold war, the predominant tendency among Japanese intellectuals was to accept and endorse the legitimacy of the communist regimes in the Eastern bloc, although they were quite vociferous in denouncing dictatorial regimes that were part of what was called the free world. Not wanting to provoke the East unnecessarily, the government did not raise issues such as the undemocratic and tyrannical nature of the regimes in the communist bloc. Besides, as far as the values agenda was concerned, the leftists were in an advantageous position, monopolizing the idea of peace as the supreme value in Japan.

In the zero sum game of the cold war, in which the top priority of the West was to maintain the precarious balance between the two blocs so that the catastrophe of nuclear war could be averted, the West initially did not have much interest in pressing its values agenda on the East. The policy cliché in those days called for peaceful coexistence between East and West; obviously, differences in their values—"Your system is awful," for example—were considered a nonissue.

It was the human rights diplomacy of President Jimmy Carter in the late 1970s that introduced the values agenda squarely in the foreign policy arena. When President Carter started to attach high priority to the human rights agenda in conducting his foreign policy, the Japanese government initially was perplexed. It was evident that if Japan rigorously pursued the human rights agenda in its dealings with neighboring countries, then its relations with them were destined to be disrupted, because at the time most of the countries in East Asia were ruled by totalitarian or dictatorial regimes. However, toward the end of the century, dynamic economic development in many countries in the region ushered in the emergence of a new middle class, which became the driving force for democratization. As a result, the sensitivity of the human rights agenda in relation to Japan's neighbors was considerably attenuated.

It was argued toward the end of Carter's presidency that his human rights policy had destabilized the regimes of many friendly countries whose support was vital to the West. In contrast to Carter, President Ronald Reagan took up the values agenda primarily in the context of the cold war. His epithet "evil empire" set the tone of the endgame of the cold war in the 1980s.

Today, the conflict in Japan between values and the national interest often is related to the use of economic sanctions against countries that perpetrate human rights abuses. Typically, "the idealist" advocates imposing sanctions, such as the suspension of economic assistance, while "the realist" argues that penalizing the country in question would substantially disrupt existing relations and would not serve the strategic interests of Japan. Whenever Europeans or Americans are at the forefront in accusing an Asian country of human rights abuses, the Asian school of Japanese identity often expresses the dissenting view. A classical case involved Japan's development assistance to China in the aftermath of the Tiananmen massacre in 1989. Japan agonized over whether to continue to suspend assistance to protest this terrible human rights abuse by Chinese authorities (the values-oriented approach) or to resume aid, defying the democratic countries of the West, because it was not in the interest of Japan to reverse its policy of economic engagement with China, which had led to a marked improvement in relations in the 1980s (the interest-oriented approach). A single standard cannot be applied to resolve this dilemma; it demands a case-by-case approach.

Apologists versus Nonapologists

In 1995, on the fiftieth anniversary of the end of World War II, the Japanese government issued a statement by Prime Minister Tomiichi Murayama, clarifying the basic position of the Japanese government regarding the war: "During a certain period in the not-too-distant past, Japan, following a mistaken national policy, advanced along the road to war, only to ensnare the Japanese people in a fateful crisis, and, through its colonial rule and aggression, caused tremendous damage and suffering to the people of many countries, particularly to those of Asian nations. In the hope that no such mistake be made in the future, I regard, in a spirit of humility, these irrefutable facts of history, and express here again my feeling of deep remorse and state my heartfelt apology."

Seven years later, one gets the impression that polarization is occurring on the history issue. For the sake of simplicity, it can be described as a clash between apologists and nonapologists, although the debate is not so much about apology per se as about a way of looking at history.

The nonapologist school of thought is not monolithic. Moderates among the nonapologists take the position that although Japan admittedly inflicted terrible pain on its Asian neighbors, it already has apologized amply and therefore should not have to repeat the apology whenever its Asian neighbors or others demand it. Besides, there is a growing sense of frustration among the younger generation, which does not see the rationale for apologizing for actions taken long before their birth. Those who take a more hardline stance contend that there was nothing morally wrong with what Japan did in the prewar era and that therefore there is no need for apology. The division between the two is defined by the question of whether and to what extent one should glorify the past. Apparently, there are more moderates than hardliners, although the latter have gotten more vociferous in recent years.

Apologists, who share the view that Japan committed terrible atrocities in the prewar era, naturally refuse to glorify the past. However, their views vary regarding the extent to which Japan should have to continue to express official apologies or offer monetary compensation to the victims of its actions.

The issue with Japan's neighbors is not about apology per se. They often stress that what they are most concerned about is whether the Japanese people have genuinely learned the lessons of history; they believe that only if the Japanese people do so can the resurgence of Japanese militarism be prevented. Whenever Japan's neighbors begin to suspect that Japan's prewar history is going to be officially glorified, for example, in the process of certifying a history textbook or when a prime minister makes an official visit to Yasukuni Shrine, a memorial to Japan's war dead, they express their strong resentment.

That the historical memory of victims of war does not easily fade was amply manifested throughout the 1990s in the former Yugoslavia, where atrocities committed by the Turks against Serbs in the fourteenth century became the driving force behind Serbian persecution of the Albanians in Kosovo. It would appear safe to assume that the much more recent memory of the atrocities committed by Japan against its neighbors in the prewar period is even less likely to fade anytime soon. Moreover, the very memory of humiliation often can become the basis of a fiercely emotional nationalism. Therefore the history issue is likely to be a truly difficult and sensitive parameter of Japan's foreign policy.

Nationalism versus Internationalism

If one is looking for a concept that can be dialectically contrasted with nationalism, perhaps "internationalism" is a candidate. In the 1980s the government of Japan adopted the notion of "internationalization" as the guiding principle of its foreign policy. The idea was to introduce systemic changes in the structure of the Japanese economy in order to facilitate the entry of foreign players into Japanese markets. At the time, foreigners were increasingly exasperated by the difficulties that they encountered in their attempts to become active participants in different sectors of the Japanese economy—including trade in goods and services, which had been handled exclusively by Japanese nationals—and direct investment in those sectors that had been closed to foreigners. Because Japan was amassing a huge trade surplus with the rest of the world, it was imperative to initiate a systemic opening up of its economy to other countries. Internationalism was conceived primarily as an approach to managing Japan's economic relations with the rest of the world.

In contrast, nationalism is difficult to define. Practically all Japanese were seized with a strong sense of nationalism while they watched the Japanese national soccer team play in the World Cup in the summer of 2002. However, such nationalism is unlikely to be relevant in the domestic debate on foreign policy. Perhaps it might make more sense to distinguish between "healthy" and "unhealthy" nationalism. But again, things can be complicated further. It is worthwhile to list some typical issues that can contribute to manifestations of nationalism.

One issue is the resentment or frustration among the Japanese people toward foreign countries and specific aspects of Japanese foreign policy that are perceived to be soft on or subservient to foreign countries. Traditionally there were two sources of frustration. One was the pressure from foreign countries, in particular the United States, to open the Japanese market. In retrospect, the process of gradual opening did not damage the dynamism of Japan's economy. However, the opening of specific sectors was pushed through under pressure from foreign countries, often the United States, rather than through efforts to convince the people that it was in the overall interest of the Japanese economy. As a result, a victim mentality persists among the Japanese, who believe that Japan is always forced to succumb to foreign pressure.

The other source of frustration is the U.S.-Japanese security arrangement, which, as discussed, the pacifists have been at the forefront in denouncing since its inception. However, some people who have a right-of-center ideological orientation, unlike the pacifists, also oppose it because they believe that the arrangement—which was based on the protector-protégé relation between the United States and Japan in the immediate aftermath of Japan's defeat—obliges Japan to remain subservient to the United States. An extreme form of this type of frustration might logically lead to a political posture similar to Gaullism, although no such trend has gathered strength thus far. Moreover, given U.S. global activism in the aftermath of 9/11, U.S. military predominance, and the U.S. proclivity to pursue a unilateralist foreign policy, the perception that Japan is subservient to the United States is likely to be exacerbated in Japan.

Serious crimes or mishaps involving American personnel stationed at U.S. military bases in Japan also contribute to the Japanese people's anger and resentment. The base issue often becomes a rallying point not only for pacifists but also for nationalists.

In a relatively new development, China also has become a focal point of frustrated or resentful nationalism, for various possible reasons: the emergence of China as a dynamic economic competitor of Japan; its sheer size, which suggests that China will become the dominant economic and military power in Asia; growing nationalism in China, which often manifests itself in anti-Japanese sentiment; the impression that China adamantly refuses to let the history issue rest; and the perception shared by many Japanese that China is eager to undermine Japan's interests. Japan's relations with China are discussed in some detail in chapter 5. Suffice it here to point out that avoiding the clash of nationalistic sentiments will remain difficult for both countries.

In any country, historical memory is a key feature of nationalism and the tendency to glorify national history is inevitable. The resentment of the nonapologists, therefore, can be described as a manifestation of nationalistic sentiment. To what extent frustrated or resentful nationalism may become a key parameter in foreign policy decisionmaking will have to be assessed carefully. Obviously, in the age of globalization any policy orientation that is averse to deepening and widening interaction with the rest of the world is bound to be a nonstarter. Therefore, dealing with the unhealthy type of nationalism, which sometimes borders on xenophobia, may become a serious priority on the national agenda. One hypothesis was that as long as unwavering confidence in the Japanese way of doing things predominated in Japan, there would not be much room for widespread nationalism of that type. But as Japan enters a historic transitional phase in which it appears that the familiar rules of the game will have to be discarded and seemingly more Darwinian "survival of the fittest" strategies accepted, it is understandable that anxiety or perhaps pessimism about the future may provide fertile ground for the growth of frustration and resentment. Of course, it is unlikely that the mood in Japan will easily swing back to the proud nationalism, bordering occasionally on hubris, of the 1980s, when the Japanese economy looked so invincible. Still, it is extremely important that the Japanese people recover some degree of confidence in the future, more specifically about their collective capacity for making the dynamic adjustments that they have made in past crises.

Obsessions about Economic Vulnerability

Ever since Japan embarked on its quest to catch up with the West following the Meiji Restoration, an obsession about the scarcity of key natural resources in Japan seems to have been deeply embedded in the national psyche. The export of manufactured products from Japan was considered to be essential in order to secure key resources and materials from abroad. The corollary of this mercantilist orientation was imperialist expansion to secure areas in the vicinity of Japan that could serve not only as markets for Japan's products but also as suppliers of various resources. In the 1930s, while Shigeru Yoshida was Japanese ambassador in London, he emphasized to key British leaders that maintaining an economic sphere of influence in northeast Asia was essential to Japan's national survival. Obviously Yoshida reasoned that since the United Kingdom had been one of the great imperial powers, its understanding or at least acquiescence in regard to Japan's actions in Manchuria and China would be highly helpful. However, one commodity that northeast Asia could not supply was oil. Japan depended on the United States for its supply of oil, which was essential to the conduct of war. Today, to prepare for war against the United States when Japan was totally dependent on the United States for oil looks like an act of lunacy. Both Japan and the United States were aware that Japan's only alternative source of oil was the Dutch East Indies—now Indonesia—and Japan's readiness to launch a military advance into the Dutch colony made it obvious that war was inevitable.

In the postwar era, Japan has suffered from two types of obsession about economic vulnerability. One, as mentioned, relates to Japan's vulnerability with regard to its supply of natural resources, in particular, oil. The other relates to its access to the export market. In particular, Japan has been haunted by the possibility of other countries forming economic blocs from which Japan might be excluded and as a result restricted in international trade.

After the end of World War II, Japan's first priority was to get back into the world market so that exports could be resumed. The U.S. government, having been convinced in the early 1950s of the strategic desirability of supporting Japanese economic reconstruction, opened the U.S. market to cheap manufactured commodities from Japan. The United States also helped Japan to join the General Agreement on Tariffs and Trade (GATT), although it took many years to overcome the reluctance of other major trading countries to give Japan full-fledged member status. The loss of the Chinese market, which used to account for roughly one-third of Japanese external trade in the prewar era, meant tremendous damage to Japanese trade. Although Prime Minister Yoshida opted for joining the "free world," one of his first actions was to attempt to resume trade with the People's Republic of China (PRC), defying arguments by some Americans officials that expanding trade between Japan and PRC would not serve the strategic interests of the free world. Yoshida's attitude toward China is discussed in chapter 5.

Joining GATT was important because its members accorded most-favored nation (MFN) status to one another across the board. As long as that principle was upheld, Japan did not have to worry about differential treatment by other countries that might be eager to restrict Japan's market access. In those days, the memory of the bloc economies of the 1930s, which had accelerated the decline of Japanese world trade, was still vivid among the Japanese; Japan therefore found the formation of the European Common Market a worrisome development. If it had been possible, Japan would have been happy to block the endeavor. It should be pointed out that Japan did not have the option of forming a similar regional association in East Asia, simply because there was no country in the region with which Japan could undertake a viable attempt at economic integration.

In the case of Europe, there was a basis for the horizontal division of labor among the countries in the region. Even though they had to make huge efforts in the 1950s and 1960s to recover from the damage that they suffered during World War II, their national economies had reached the stage of advanced industrialization. The formation of a single market that makes it possible for European countries to benefit from economies of scale by trading manufactured commodities with each other has become the key factor in their economic growth since the 1960s. In contrast, Japan's trade relations with its East Asian neighbors was characterized by the vertical division of labor: Japan exported manufactured goods to and imported primary commodities from its neighbors, because of the differences in their respective stages of economic development. No economies of scale could be achieved by forming a single market among the countries in the region.

Eventually, perhaps inspired by the success of the European endeavor, the formation of free trade areas became the vogue in various parts of the world. Japan always watched this process with the uncomfortable feeling that the ideal trade order of GATT, which was based on the global application of MFN status, was being eroded by the regional free trade schemes, to the detriment of Japan. Of course it can be argued in hindsight that Japan's trade with Europe has expanded markedly as a result of the dynamic European economic growth that followed regional integration. Still, the fear that Japan might be left behind in the international trend toward regional integration remains a key parameter of its foreign policy.

Japan's other sense of vulnerability relates to the supply of oil. In the post–World War II era, Japan's dependence on oil from the Middle East remained extremely high, and Japanese companies attempted to exploit oil deposits in the Gulf area. However, Japan's tacit and optimistic assumption was that since the major U.S. oil companies were its main suppliers of oil, any possible disruption of supply would be effectively prevented by the United States and perhaps the United Kingdom. It was not until the embargo by oil-producing countries in the Gulf area in the aftermath of the Yom Kippur War in 1973 that Japan suddenly awakened to its vulnerability in regard to its supply of oil. The oil embargo shattered the Japanese people's confidence and expectation that Japan would continue along the path toward unprecedented prosperity. Although the embargo was not effectively enforced, the huge hikes in the price of oil that ensued further intensified the Japanese sense of vulnerability. At the time, the sense of crisis was shared by all the democratic industrial countries, so much so that the first G-6 summit meeting, officially called the Summit of the Industrial Democracies, was convened at the initiative of France in the fall of 1975.

Following another round of oil shortages toward the end of the 1970s after the turmoil in Iran, issues related to the oil supply, such as the stability of the Persian Gulf region, came to top the national agenda not only in Japan but in practically all the major countries. However, as time passed it became evident, to the relief of many, that even in the case of oil the market mechanism worked and the likelihood of oil embargoes diminished markedly. Japan made a nationwide effort to reduce its dependence on oil from the Gulf throughout the latter half of the 1970s. (In

1970, oil accounted for 71.9 percent of total energy consumption in Japan, and 84.6 percent of that oil came from the Gulf. By 1985, those numbers had dropped to 56.3 percent and 68.8 percent, respectively.)

Still, the oil crisis—later called the "oil shock"—was the first instance since the end of World War II in which the Japanese acutely felt their vulnerability to dependence on foreign resources. Its imprint on the national psyche will not fade easily and may quickly reappear if another crisis affecting the oil supply should erupt.

2 | *Security Ties between Japan and the United States*

In a memorable success for both victors and vanquished, following the end of World War II Japan and Germany began to adopt the values and ideals of their former adversaries and eventually formed security arrangements with the United States that have been pillars of peace and security—for more than half a century—in marked contrast to events in the aftermath of World War I. The decisive factor was the advent of the cold war, in which adversarial relations developed among the victors, with the United States and the West Europeans on one side and the Soviet Union and its satellites on the other. In the newly emerging zero-sum game of the cold war, the United States began to regard the economic potential of Japan and Germany as a huge asset to the free world and the alignment of either nation with the communist bloc as a devastating loss. But even before the cold war began, the United States was fully aware of the lesson of Versailles—that the revanchism of the victor may be the best way of ensuring another war in the future. The first priority of the United States, therefore, was not so much to impose punitive measures on its former enemies as to give them an opportunity to work for the reconstruction of their country, as long as the systemic causes of their militarism could be eradicated completely. And both Japan and West Germany accepted that opportunity. Had Japan fiercely objected to U.S. policies during the occupation and tried to maintain the remnants of militarism in the immediate aftermath of defeat, the course of history would have been different. That Japan decided instead to accept the vast reform agenda that the United States was eager to carry out allowed the United States to focus on ensuring Japan's security instead of ensuring its own security against Japan, and to treat Japan as a strategic asset in the emerging cold war.

One wonders how the Allied Powers would have reacted if Japan had procrastinated in implementing the terms of surrender and secretly engaged in developing nuclear weapons, as Saddam Hussein did after the end of the Persian Gulf war in 1991. It is interesting to note that, following the defeat of Hussein's regime by the United States and its allies in May 2003, the postwar reconstruction of Japan reportedly is being considered as a model for the current reconstruction effort in Iraq. Although the situation in Japan in 1945 was vastly different from that of Iraq in 2003, one can say at least that far-sighted planning by the United States made the ensuing stability and economic recovery of its former adversaries possible.

The fascinating historical process that culminated in the signing of the San Francisco Peace Treaty and the Security Treaty between the United States and Japan in 1951 is covered in many books. This chapter does not attempt to elaborate further on the actual course of history; rather, it reflects on the hypothetical as well as the realistic options available to decisionmakers at that time—and perhaps more important, on the extent to which new options may present themselves half a century later. Certainly it does not make much sense to imagine alternative courses of history, speculating, for example, on what U.S. policy regarding the security of Japan would have been if the Soviets had continued to behave nicely. Without the advent of the cold war, the UN Security Council would likely have functioned as envisioned in Chapter 7 of the UN Charter. Japan would have assumed that the UN would ensure its national security, and there would have been no U.S. push for Japanese rearmament and no security agreement between Japan and the United States. And indeed, that was the assumption of the Japanese government toward the end of the 1940s. However, the advent of the cold war, and in particular the eruption of the Korean War in 1950, utterly shattered Japanese expectations that the UN would be able to guarantee international security. Still, during negotiations with the United States to end the occupation, the Japanese sought to define the security arrangement with the United States as a provisional measure justified as the exercise of the right of self-defense in accordance with Article 51 of the UN Charter, pending eventual action by the Security Council to restore peace and security.

It should be noted that the expectation that the UN would someday have the authority and capability to ensure the peace and security of the whole world survived in Japan through the cold war. Interestingly, this expectation was shared not only by the pacifists, who disliked the alliance with the United States, but also by the realists, who believed that Japan could and should offer its own personnel to serve in a UN force in the event that one was organized, since such an action would be perfectly permissible under the constitution.

Prime Minister Shigeru Yoshida often is quoted as describing the Korean War as "kamikaze" (the wind of God). Certainly it gave a huge boost to the Japanese economy, as Japan supplied the United States with a massive amount of the goods and services that were essential to the conduct of the war. But apart from the economic benefits, the war improved the prime minister's position in his effort to negotiate the end of the occupation by concluding the peace treaty with the Allied Powers.

Theoretically speaking, what options did Yoshida have before concluding the peace treaty and the security treaty, simultaneously, in San Francisco in 1951? Obviously, the negotiations were not between equal sovereign countries, but between victor and vanquished; the options, therefore, were limited. Certainly the cold war had enhanced the strategic value of Japan as an important member of the free world. That fact strengthened the effectiveness of Yoshida's gambit in resisting U.S. demands—for example, for Japan's prompt rearmament—by stressing the imminent danger of the takeover of Japan by the communists and other leftists if economic deprivation worsened. However, the argument that "Japan might drift toward the communist bloc unless you help" was not a viable alternative; as far as Yoshida, a staunch anticommunist, was concerned, opting for the communist bloc was totally out of question. His stance was based not only on his ideological disdain of communism but also on his conviction that Japan's economic recovery and national security could be secured only by joining the free world. Even though the Bretton Woods system was still in its infancy, it is evident that there was no practical alternative other than to try to gain maximum economic benefit from that system.

The leftists insisted that Japan should not conclude a peace treaty with the Allied Powers until all the powers, including the Soviet Union and the People's Republic of China, were represented in the talks. This stance called for what was described as an "all-embracing peace" rather than a "separate peace"—a treaty with the United States. The leftists fiercely opposed a separate treaty on the grounds that it would mean that Japan was taking the U.S. side in the cold war and thereby becoming an enemy of the communist bloc, which in their view was wrong and dangerous for Japan. This was a typical manifestation of the pacifists' fear of entanglement in war. As far as Yoshida was concerned, joining the U.S. side was precisely what he intended to do. He asserted that to insist on the pursuit of an all-embracing peace when the cold war was intensifying was totally unrealistic and derided the idea as "an attempt to pick a flower in a mirror."

In the autumn of 1950, during preparations for the treaty talks, a team of advisers submitted to Prime Minister Yoshida what might be termed the idealists' proposal, the gist of which called for the complete disarmament of Japan and the Korean Peninsula and for arms reduction by four powers—the United States, the Soviet Union, the People's Republic of China, and the United Kingdom—in the Far East. The idea was to ensure Japan's security without rearming Japan. However, Yoshida refrained from tabling the proposal, which, when the same four powers were engaged in a deadly war on the Korean Peninsula, was bound to be a nonstarter.

That episode calls to mind the option of the "unarmed neutrality" of Japan. Before the advent of the cold war, General Douglas MacArthur once suggested that Japan should aim at becoming the "Switzerland of the Orient." It is doubtful that he envisioned Japan equipped with the Swiss Army's legendary defense capability; instead, what he had in mind was a totally demilitarized, neutral Japan. Many Japanese loved the idea of being Switzerland in the Orient—that may be one reason why Switzerland has been one of the most popular countries in Japanese opinion polls since the end of the war.

The pacifists advocated Japan's unarmed neutrality. However, the neutrality or total demilitarization of a country is infeasible unless it is guaranteed by all surrounding powers. Without a guarantee, the peace and security of a country can be seriously compromised, and the end result may well be intervention or invasion by powers eager to take over the country or preempt its takeover by rival powers. In the regional power game of the early 1950s, if Japan had opted for neutrality without U.S. acquiescence the move would have been seen by the United States as a hostile action. And in that case, Japan would have been compelled to think seriously about its security vis-à-vis the United States.

Today, many Japanese tend to overlook the fact that in the postwar era, unlike in the first phase of Japan's modernization, from 1868 to 1945, Japan no longer had to worry about the possibility of the United States becoming an adversary. It sounds so obvious that it can easily be taken for granted. Still, that fact was a result of the difficult decision-making involved in picking one option instead of others that were advocated by the pacifists and idealists and had considerable resonance among the Japanese people.

The crucial element in the U.S.-Japanese security treaty of 1951 was Japan's agreement that the United States could continue to maintain military bases in Japan, where, at the time the treaty went into effect in 1952, 110,000 U.S. forces were stationed. The opposition charged that the new treaty was nothing but a U.S. ploy to continue the occupation of Japan. Today the consensus of historians is that Prime Minister Yoshida considered the continued use of bases a crucial card to play in resisting American pressure for Japan's substantial rearmament. It was equally evident that the U.S. forces stationed in Japan would fight to defend Japan in case of armed attack by other countries, notably the Soviet Union. Article I of the treaty specifies:

> With the entry into force of the Treaty, Japan permits the right to deploy the Army, the Navy, and the Air Force of the United States within and in the vicinity of Japan and the United States accepts this right. . . . This Force may be used to contribute to the international peace and security in the Far East, and . . . to contribute to the security of Japan against armed attack from outside.

A decade later, under the leadership of Prime Minister Shinsuke Kishi, the Treaty of Security and Mutual Cooperation between Japan and the United States of America was concluded, replacing the security treaty of 1951. In the new treaty of 1960, the legal obligation of the United States to protect Japan was clearly stipulated and the requirement of prior consultation regarding the use of bases was defined so that the notion of unrestrained use could be dispelled.

Throughout the history of the U.S.-Japanese security arrangement, which has been in effect for more than half a century, the base issue has always been the key pillar. In essence, the United States assumes the legal obligation to defend Japan, and Japan permits the United States to maintain bases in Japan. This structure often is described as asymmetrical in that the defense commitment is not mutual, given Japan's constitutional constraint against the exercise of collective self-defense. The U.S. defense commitment is considered to be balanced by the U.S. right to maintain bases in Japan not only for the defense of Japan but also for U.S. operations to ensure peace and security in the Far East—the latter a considerable strategic asset to the United States during both the cold war era and its aftermath. Naturally, the pacifists opposed the very idea of offering the use of bases to the United States, and the precise location of the geographical boundaries of "the Far East" often has been a contentious issue in the parliament. If, for example, U.S. forces stationed in Japan are sent somewhere else, such as the Persian Gulf region, the pacifists will question the legality of the deployment under the treaty because the region is outside the Far East. Also, according to the treaty of 1960, certain aspects of the use of bases—namely, any important changes in the deployment of U.S. forces, any important changes in the equipment used (for example, use of nuclear weapons, which is categorically refused by Japan), and military operations conducted from Japan—are subject to prior consultation with Japan, and debate has frequently erupted over the extent of prior consultation.

What sorts of alternatives were available to Japan in the formative phase of the security arrangement? As mentioned, Prime Minister Yoshida played the base use card to resist U.S. pressure for rearmament. Yoshida also was probably well aware of the deterrent effect of letting the United States continue to use bases in Japan, thereby assuring automatic U.S. involvement in the defense of Japan in the event of armed attack. If Japan had decided to rearm, the base use card might not have been needed. However, in view of the domestic climate in Japan, including the economic feasibility of sustaining a military buildup as well as the possibility of strong popular opposition, it seems in hindsight that substantial rearmament never constituted a realistic option. In any event, in 1950 Yoshida launched a modest rearmament initiative by creating what was initially called the Police Reserve Force, which included 5,000 officers; this became the Japanese Self-Defense Force in 1954.

Another option was to try to obtain a defense commitment from the United States without offering the use of bases—or at least to hold any offer until the final stage of negotiations. If Japan had not been constrained by the constitution and had been ready to accept a mutual defense commitment—that is, if it had been ready to fight with the United States if hostilities broke out in East Asia—it might not have been necessary to offer the use of bases. Security ties based on mutual defense could have been possible, assuming that the huge disparity between the two countries in terms of their actual defense capability was not taken into account. But because that was simply impossible, it would not have been a plausible opening gambit for Japan to declare to the United States, "After the termination of the occupation, you are to withdraw your troops from Japan but nevertheless assume the legal obligation to protect us. Meanwhile, we will not carry out the rearmament that you expect of us, and, as you know, constitutionally we are not allowed to fight with you, except for our own defense." One may be tempted to argue that since the strategic value of Japan to the United States was so high in the zero-sum game of the cold war, regardless of what Japan was or was not prepared to offer, the United States had no option but to defend Japan. However, that type of bluff, so to speak, by Japan would have fatally frayed the basic fabric of goodwill and trust between the two countries. In any negotiations, an element of bluffing and the use of assorted red herrings are common. Still, in the course of negotiating a defense commitment, for which mutual trust is essential, countries should not take the risk of destroying that trust lightly.

A Rough Sketch of Events after the Security Treaty of 1960

Prime Minister Hayato Ikeda took power after the resignation of Prime Minister Kishi, who managed to conclude the treaty of 1960 in the midst of political upheaval (the high point of which came when a huge crowd of demonstrators broke onto the Diet campus to protest the new treaty). Ikeda succeeded in restoring relative calm in Japanese politics by putting the pursuit of economic growth at the top of the national agenda. His political platform, which was based on doubling the national income, and his posture—"As far as the economy goes, trust me"—worked effectively.

After the treaty of 1960 established the framework of Japan's security arrangement with the United States, the basic task for successive leaders of the Liberal Democratic Party was to maintain the arrangement's effectiveness in the face of pacifist opposition. The clash between the pacifists (the opposition) and the realists (the government) persisted with varying intensity. A rough description of Japanese political culture at that time suggests that the majority of the population supported the LDP for its success in fostering dynamic economic growth, while finding considerable appeal in the pacifist posture as well.

Various developments affected Japan's security environment between the late 1960s and the end of the 1980s. In the 1960s, the United States was bogged down in the Vietnam War. Nobody was quite sure to what extent the domino theory was going to be relevant in Southeast Asia; still, the situation looked extremely precarious. The base issue, in the context of the U.S. action in Vietnam, was hotly debated in parliament.

It was in this setting that Japan had to negotiate the reversion of Okinawa from U.S. to Japanese control. Throughout the occupation, the United States had taken for granted its indefinite retention of Okinawa, which was a crucial base for the forward deployment of U.S. forces. During the early occupation, even those in the United States who envisioned a thoroughly demilitarized Japan assumed that the handling of Okinawa would be different. In the 1960s, with the intensification of the war in Vietnam and the worrisome uncertainties in the Korean Peninsula and the Taiwan Strait, Okinawa remained of crucial strategic importance to the United States.

The historic negotiation of the reversion of Okinawa is well documented. The disposition of the U.S. bases in Okinawa was the crux of the issue. As set forth in the Joint Statement of Prime Minister Eisaku Sato and President Richard Nixon in 1969, the reversion should be accomplished "without impairing the security of the Far East including Japan." The leaders agreed that the existing security arrangement between the countries "should be applied to Okinawa without modification thereof" and that "the reversion should not hinder the effective execution of the international obligations assumed by the United States for the defense of countries in the Far East including Japan." It was a truly commendable achievement of the two countries that the reversion of Okinawa was accomplished without calling for a different treatment of the bases in Okinawa.

Henry Kissinger's spectacular gambit in initiating rapprochement with China in 1971 changed the contours of power politics in Asia. And in that context, Japan normalized its relations with China in 1972. As the Soviet Union had become a serious threat to Chinese security by the end of the 1960s, China no longer raised much opposition to the security arrangement between the United States and Japan. In fact, in the early 1980s China even adopted a posture of acquiescence toward it, since it could effectively serve as a deterrent to Soviet aggression.

Perhaps the détente during the 1970s—which made direct military invasion by the Soviets look less likely—had the effect of reducing the Japanese fear of entanglement in war that drove the pacifist opposition in earlier periods. Still, the debate in both the Diet and much of the media was dominated by the clash between pacifists and realists. Against that background, Japan's defense was planned to deal only with limited invasion; any full-scale invasion, presumably by the Soviet Union, would be dealt with by the United States, which was expected to rush to Japan's defense. During this period, defense expenditures remained about 1 percent of the gross national product (GNP). In later years, the 1 percent ceiling became the gauge of Japan's defense effort.

The fall of Saigon and the victory of the communist forces in Indochina—and the ensuing image of a defeated United States, whose national psyche seemed to be badly bruised—certainly had an impact on domestic politics in Japan. However, the event that awakened the Japanese sense of vulnerability in those years was related not to the cold war, but to the oil crisis in the aftermath of the Yom Kippur War, in 1973. By the beginning of the 1970s, the Japanese people's memory of the painful economic deprivation that the country had suffered immediately after the end of World War II had faded. They had begun to assume that regardless of external developments, such as the deteriorating war in Vietnam, Japan's future prosperity was ensured. They were all the more shocked, therefore, to realize the vulnerability of Japan's economy to the unexpected disruption of the supply of crude oil from the Middle East following the Arab oil embargo.

The concept of comprehensive security, which came into vogue at that time, was a result of this acute sense of economic vulnerability. There was thought to be no point in concentrating on national security in its narrow sense, such as the adequacy of Japan's defense capability or the effectiveness of its security arrangement with the United States, since the disruption of the supply of a key commodity such as oil could, in effect, put an end to the very existence of Japan. "Comprehensive," therefore, became a key word. Besides, the Japanese still seemed to have some allergy to handling the security issue per se. The need to take stock of all aspects of the nation's vulnerability—not only its military capability but also its access to natural resources—was far more convincing and palatable to the majority of the Japanese.

The end of the 1970s brought with it what was described at the time as a renewal of the cold war. The acquisition of naval bases in Vietnam by the Soviets in 1979 was thought to signal the emergence of a new strategic parameter in East Asia, and the subsequent Soviet invasion of Afghanistan toward the end of 1979 totally destroyed the remnants of détente. Affirmation of solidarity with the West became an important item on the national agenda, and the boycott of the Olympic Games in Moscow in 1980 became a litmus test of that solidarity. In late 1979, even before the invasion of Afghanistan, Japan had encountered difficulty over Iran, which used to be an important source of oil even after the Islamic revolution under Ayatollah Khomeini. In the middle of U.S. anguish over the hostage crisis in Tehran, it was disclosed that Japan continued to purchase Iranian oil. This news immediately kindled anti-Japanese fury in the United States. Although a crisis was swiftly sidestepped when both the United States and Japan took various measures to reaffirm their solidarity, it was an important lesson for Japan. In early 1980, Prime Minister Masayoshi Ohira declared that "Japan was ready to share the pain and burden with the United States."

In hindsight, the Reagan administration ushered in the end game of the cold war, although nobody had the slightest premonition that the end was near. The administration feared at the outset that the military capability of the Soviets might eventually surpass that of the United States, and its first priority was to strengthen the military capability of the United States and its allies. The strengthening of the JSDF's ability to share the defense burden with the United States, in particular the defense of a sea lane roughly 1,000 miles in length that extended from Japan to an area north of the Philippines, topped the U.S.-Japanese agenda. The United States attached tremendous importance to the protection of this sea lane because, in the event of an attack on Japan, it would have to be used to transport troops and materiel.

In one interesting episode, on the occasion of an official visit to the United States, Prime Minister Zenko Suzuki's use of the term "the alliance" in describing the U.S.-Japanese security arrangement triggered an uproar in Japan. Before that, the Japanese government had refrained from using the term because it could be interpreted to indicate a more aggressive arrangement and was likely to be fiercely attacked by the pacifists. It was Prime Minister Yasuhiro Nakasone who forcefully voiced a policy of support for President Reagan by stating on the occasion of his first official visit to the United States in early 1983 that Japan and the United States were bound by a shared destiny, and later by taking the lead in affirming at the G-7 Summit at Williamsburg that "the security of the West was indivisible."

In the history of the U.S.-Japanese security arrangement, the truly defining moment was the signing of the 1951 security treaty, which was essential for terminating the occupation. Thereafter, much of the effort of successive Japanese governments has gone toward maintaining deterrence, which has been based on the security ties and the defense capability of the JSDF. It is true that other options, such as unarmed neutrality, were advocated by the pacifists, and their ideas had considerable resonance among the people of Japan. However, no truly meaningful alternative for ensuring Japan's security could have arisen during the cold war, unless, of course, Japan was prepared to consider the option of joining the communist bloc and having the United States as an adversary. Later, Prime Minister Kishi reportedly defined the salient feature of conservative orthodoxy (hoshu-honryuu) in Japanese politics as the maintenance of good relations with the United States.

However, because the security arrangement was not negotiated between two equal, sovereign countries but between victor and vanquished to terminate the occupation of the latter by the former, some sense of frustration and humiliation persisted among the Japanese. Those sentiments resembled somewhat the sentiments of the Japanese in the early Meiji era toward the "unequal treaties" with the Western powers and often manifested themselves in the criticism that the government doggedly followed U.S. policy. Nor were such feelings the monopoly of the pacifists; they were shared by the Asian identity school described in chapter 1. Occasionally, one gets the impression that in Japan any policy that openly opposes U.S. policy is the surest way to get applause. Obviously, Japan should forcefully assert its national interest in its dealings with the United States, including the management of the security arrangement; it can be argued, however, that often U.S. policy was more or less in line with Japan's national interest. Moreover, the bottom line in maintaining the security ties should be to refrain from doing things that harm the United States, inasmuch as mutual support is what the alliance is all about.

Apart from unarmed neutrality, the notion of "independently oriented defense," a close approximation of Gaullism in France, occasionally surfaced in Japan, although it never predominated. In the early period of the security agreement, Ichiro Hatoyama, the political rival of Yoshida, advocated what was called the "independent defense policy." The gist of the policy was to revise the constitution so that the rearmament of Japan could be formally undertaken, and it was intended to play up the contrast with the incremental approach taken by Prime Minister Yoshida in creating the JSDF without revising the constitution. Hatoyama's proposal embodied the views of the conservatives, who had considerable reservations regarding the posture of Yoshida, which in their opinion was too pro-American. However, as the buildup of the JSDF began to get under way and after Hatoyama became prime minister in 1954, the enthusiasm for constitutional revision subsided, and with it the call for an independent defense policy.

In later years some argued for a Gaullist defense doctrine. However, since the basic tenet of Gaullism was the refusal to rely on the nuclear umbrella provided by the United States and since Japan had no realistic nuclear options, it was never a persuasive alternative. It is interesting to note that in Japan the credibility of the U.S. defense commitment did not become a key issue in parliamentary debate, in marked contrast with Western Europe, where U.S. credibility had always been the dominant concern among members of NATO. In particular, the question of "coupling and decoupling"—that is, whether the United States was prepared to risk a Soviet nuclear attack on its own soil to defend its European allies surfaced again and again. Perhaps because the focus of the debate between the pacifists and realists had always been the fear of entanglement in war, the credibility issue did not claim center stage in Japan.

The Changing Role of the JSDF: The Gulf War and Thereafter

Japan's post–cold war security agenda has been characterized by a series of legislative measures authorizing the government to engage the JSDF in various noncombat activities outside Japan, reflecting the desirability of playing an active role in maintaining international peace and security in the new era. Throughout the process of redefining the role and mission of the JSDF, debate between the pacifists and realists has been continual, as it was during the cold war; however, the international situation has been markedly different.

First, when the fear of entanglement in warfare was stressed during the cold war era, what was envisaged was the possibility of Japan being dragged into deadly hostilities between the communist bloc and the free world. In the post–cold war era, hostilities are not likely to result from bipolar confrontation but from various types of despicable and sometimes tragic behavior on the part of rogue states and nonstate actors, against whom the international community as a whole must take deterrent or remedial action to restore peace. To refuse to work for such an international endeavor because of the fear of entanglement hardly sounds convincing. Moreover, it is in the interests of Japan to redress any disruption of peace and security through the concerted action of like-minded countries in the international community.

The first challenge for Japan was the Persian Gulf war of 1991. It was clear from the outset that since so many other countries had sent their own military personnel for various missions, not necessarily combat, the presence of Japanese personnel was highly desirable. The argument might have appalled the pacifists, but it seemed very important in terms of solidarity that Japan share a certain amount of the risk with other like-minded nations. However, because the Japanese system was not well prepared to address this type of challenge, the government did not send any personnel except those on the minesweepers that were sent to the Gulf after hostilities ended.

In the fall of 1990, when the use of force during a multinational campaign to liberate Kuwait looked inevitable, the government tried to enact a law that would permit the JSDF to engage in noncombat activities to support the effort. However, the government could not overcome the various pacifist arguments opposing the legislation. There was considerable psychological resistance to anything related to deployment of the military, even in a noncombat capacity, and the pacifists began to treat the United States as if it, instead of Iraq, were the aggressor, eager to launch a war.

As a result, the government attached a condition to its $9 billion contribution to the multinational force, stipulating that it could not be used to purchase weapons. Moreover, it decided that in assisting transport operations of the multinational force, Japan could transport only non-military goods. Such were the effects of the battle between the pacifists and realists on the scope and substance of Japan's contribution to the international effort. Although Japan contributed $13 billion to the operations of the multinational forces, many realists felt humiliated because Japan had not sent personnel, and that sense of humiliation became the driving force behind subsequent legislative measures regarding the JSDF.

The 1991 Gulf war set an important precedent regarding the role of the UN Security Council. If the UN force envisaged in Chapter 7 of the UN Charter had existed, perhaps Iraq's invasion of Kuwait would have presented a classic opportunity to deploy the force to maintain international order. However, since the UN force was nonexistent, what may be called the second-best solution was attempted. The Security Council adopted Resolution 660, which authorized UN member states to take every measure necessary to redress the situation caused by Iraq's invasion. Thus the use of force against Iraq by the multinational force was authorized and legally justified. In later years, Resolution 660 was frequently invoked when a multinational force was required to deal with various regional crises.

In Japan, the constitutional question regarding participation in the UN force proposed in Chapter 7 of the UN Charter remains unsettled. The government's position has been that a decision on whether the JSDF can join such a force must wait until the force is actually created. Ichiro Ozawa, current leader of the Liberal Party, has been an influential advocate of taking an assertive posture on the defense issue. In his view, JSDF's participation, far from being prohibited by the constitution, accords precisely with its spirit. However, it seems unlikely that agreement will be reached in the foreseeable future among the major powers on the creation of a UN force, given the reluctance of many countries to entrust their own forces to the command of an international organization. Not all major states with an effective military capability have the same opinion of the worthiness of shedding the blood of their soldiers in dealing with a particular crisis, since the stakes for each state are bound to vary depending on its national interests.

Japan urgently needs to define to what extent the JSDF can be engaged, within the constitutional constraints, in future support missions when formation of a multinational force is authorized by the UN to deal with threats to international peace and security. A breakthrough regarding Japan's participation in UN peacekeeping operations (PKO) was achieved in 1992, when a law authorizing cooperation in international peacekeeping efforts was enacted after long and heated debate in the Diet. Because the law would pave the way for dispatching Japanese military forces abroad for the first time since the end of World War II, the pacifists resorted to all sorts of arguments to prevent its passage.

After passage, the pacifists reprised their admonitions against entanglement, lamenting that at last Japan was on the slippery slope to war. Although no other countries that had sent troops for peacekeeping operations in the past were eventually entangled in war—and for that matter, entanglement in hostilities of the cold war type could hardly be envisaged—the pacifists regarded the law as the dangerous first step to Japan's military involvement overseas.

The government's position was that engaging in peacekeeping activities was in no way envisaged to include the use of force and therefore was within the constitutional constraint; however, the pacifists pointed out that the JSDF might be forced to engage in battle during a peacekeeping operation. At one stage the debate in the Diet was bogged down by the question of how the JSDF would react in the case of ambush. The pacifists maintained that since the JSDF would have to fight back, they would become engaged in the very use of force that was prohibited by the constitution.

To help allay the pacifists' fears, the law was drafted in such a way that the possibility of the use of force in the course of a peacekeeping operation was eliminated. Five conditions were placed on participation in peacekeeping operations by the JSDF:

—all parties in the conflict must have agreed to a cease-fire

—all parties in the conflict must have accepted Japan's participation in peacekeeping operations

—the PKO forces must maintain strict impartiality in performing their duties

—the JSDF must withdraw immediately upon any breakdown of the conditions set forth above

—the use of weapons is permitted only in the extremely limited case of self-defense.

It was decided that for the time being a moratorium would be placed on any proposals to dispatch the JSDF as infantry in a peacekeeping force, for example, to police a cease-fire agreement; thus the mission of the JSDF was confined mainly to providing logistical support. Only in the autumn of 2001, in the aftermath of the terrorist attacks of 9/11, did the Diet modify the PKO law so that the JSDF could perform infantry missions during peacekeeping operations.

Japan's first peacekeeping operation was in Cambodia, immediately after enactment of the PKO law. As Japan had invested a considerable amount of diplomatic capital in the restoration of peace in Cambodia, it was of great significance that a Japanese team should actively contribute to the peace of the country, which had suffered so much since the early 1970s. The Japanese people gradually became receptive to the notion of sending the JSDF abroad for noncombat missions to support cooperative efforts to maintain international peace and security. According to the polls, a considerable percentage of the Japanese expressed support for dispatching minesweepers to the Persian Gulf in 1991, after the end of the war.

Other polling data showed the same trend regarding peacekeeping operations. The percentage of those responding that Japan should not participate was 8.6 percent in 1994; by 2001 it had dropped to 1.8 percent. The percentage of those responding that Japan should minimize its participation was 25 percent in 1994; it had dropped to 10.4 percent in 2001. The percentage of those who preferred to maintain the existing level of PKO participation was 43.1 percent in 1994 and 48.5 percent in 2001. And the percentage of those who preferred more active participation doubled from 15.5 percent in 1994 to 31.2 percent in 2001.[1]

The mid-1990s were characterized by rising tension in the Korean Peninsula and the reaffirmation of the security ties between the United States and Japan. Japan's position in regard to the Korean peninsula is discussed in chapter 4, but two points should be briefly mentioned here in the context of the security agenda. First, as tension heightened in 1993–94 over the possible development of nuclear weapons by North Korea, there was an urgent need to explore the extent to which Japan could offer support activities to U.S. forces if hostilities erupted in the Korean Peninsula. Second, the government also had to study what possible steps Japan could take to ensure the effectiveness of any economic sanctions that might be imposed on North Korea by the UN Security Council. In particular, the government had to consider to what extent Japan should engage the JSDF or the Maritime Safety Agency, the equivalent of the U.S. Coast Guard, in interdicting sea cargo related to North Korea if an embargo was imposed. In the event, tension was defused after President Jimmy Carter visited North Korea and North Korea agreed to give up the construction of a plutonium nuclear reactor in exchange for a light-water reactor to be constructed under the Korean Peninsula Energy Development Organization (KEDO) agreement.

Meanwhile the first issue, the extent of Japan's support for U.S. forces engaged in military operations, remained an important priority that was eventually elaborated in guidelines developed by Japan and the United

---

1. "Public Opinion Poll on Foreign Policy," Office of Public Information, Cabinet Office of the Japanese government, February 4, 2002.

States in 1997 and clarified in a law enacted in 1999 relating to the measures to be taken to maintain Japan's peace and security "in the situation surrounding Japan"(this phrase has become established legal jargon describing circumstances in the vicinity of Japan that affect its security).

The Redefinition of the U.S.-Japanese Security Arrangement

The security ties between the United States and Japan were essentially a result of the cold war. Therefore, it was perhaps inevitable that both countries would begin to reflect on the rationale for those ties in the post–cold war era. It is easier to legitimize an alliance as long as there is a clear-cut adversary, such as the Soviets in the cold war. However, the cold war was over, and the Soviet threat had disappeared. Nonetheless, in the mid-1990s both countries fairly swiftly came to the conclusion that it would be in their mutual interest to continue their security arrangement. The United States reasoned that since it had to be prepared to address various types of future threats, it was essential to maintain a military presence in Asia Pacific and that the effectiveness of its presence depended on having solid security ties with Japan. (According to a U.S. Department of Defense review published in 1993, four types of threat existed: proliferation of weapons of mass destruction; regional threats such as North Korea and Iraq; threats to democracy and reform; and threats to U.S. economic interests.)[2] As for Japan, a continued U.S. presence in Asia Pacific would effectively deter the emergence of future threats in the region; put another way, without the United States, Japan would have to grapple single-handedly with any destabilization of the security environment in East Asia. The two countries therefore affirmed in the Japan–United States Joint Declaration on Security—subtitled "Alliance for the 21st Century"—that their existing security arrangement remained "the cornerstone for achieving common security objectives, and for maintaining a stable and prosperous environment for the Asia-Pacific region as we enter the twenty-first century."

During the cold war, a crucial assumption was that in the event of hostilities between the United States and the Soviet Union, Soviet troops stationed in the Far East were likely to invade northern Japan, most probably Hokkaido. With the end of the cold war, however, attention shifted from the possibility of a direct attack on Japan to events in the vicinity of

2. U.S. Department of Defense, *The Bottom-Up Defense*, September 1, 1993.

Japan that could seriously affect the nation's security, such as the situation in regard to North Korea. Japan was acutely aware that the extent of its support for U.S. forces was of crucial importance to the credibility of U.S.-Japanese security ties. Often cited was a scenario in which a Japanese navy ship refuses to fight to defend a U.S. navy ship under attack in the vicinity because of the constitutional constraint against the right of collective self-defense, although such a refusal might very well spell the end of the security ties between the two countries. It was jokingly suggested that the only way out of this legal quagmire would be to persuade the attacking ship to shoot at the Japanese ship so that it could exercise its right of individual self-defense.

A more serious challenge from a practical standpoint was to sort out to what extent Japan could offer logistical support for U.S. forces, and new guidelines announced in 1997 outlined permitted support activities (see box on page 40). The items listed refer to Japan's support for U.S. forces engaged in military operations outside Japan. In addition, it was agreed that cooperative activities in two areas would be promoted.

The first area included relief efforts for refugees and other victims, search-and-rescue operations, evacuation of each country's own nationals, and measures related to the effective implementation of sanctions imposed by the UN Security Council. Although these activities were supposed to be carried out independently by each country, cooperation between the two was deemed highly desirable. The second area related to activities such as minesweeping and use of airspace and sea transport lanes, for which coordination of operations was desirable.

To ensure that all these activities were carried out smoothly, promptly, and effectively, a vast amount of preparatory work by both sides was needed. It was also necessary to pass legislation authorizing the government to carry out the activities. Authorizing legislation was enacted in 1999, after lengthy debate in the Diet. The pacifist opposition was not at all convinced of the validity of the rationale for engaging the JSDF in the support activities permitted by the law. In their view, it was another dangerous ploy to expand the role of the JSDF, and they believed that supporting U.S. forces would seriously increase the risk of Japan's entanglement in war. The realists—the government supporters—naturally took the position that to support U.S. actions addressing a threat in the vicinity of Japan would be in Japan's national interest.

Thus the debate again took the form of a classic battle of legalism. The definition of "use of force" was revisited again. As mentioned in

Permitted Logistical Support Activities

—Use of facilities

Use of JSDF facilities as well as civilian seaports and airports by U.S. forces for transport purposes and for the unloading, reloading, and storage of goods and personnel

Extension of the operating hours of the facilities referred to above

Use of airfields of the JSDF by the U.S. Air Force

Use of exercise and training areas by U.S. forces

Right to build offices and accommodations at U.S. bases in Japan

—Rear area support

Supply
To supply goods (excluding weapons and ammunition) and fuel (including lubricant and other oil) to U.S. aircraft and ships at JSDF facilities as well as civilian seaports and airports and to U.S. bases in Japan

Transport
Land, sea, and air transport of personnel, goods, and fuel in Japan
Sea transport of personnel, goods, and fuel to U.S. ships on high seas
Use of vehicles and cranes for transport as described above

Maintenance
Maintenance and repair of U.S. aircraft, ships, and vehicles
Provision of spare parts and maintenance materials

Medical treatment
Medical treatment and transport of wounded in Japan
Provision of medical supplies and equipment

Guard operations
Guard U.S. bases and carry out surveillance of the surrounding seas
Guard transport routes in Japan
Exchange information related to security

Communication
Secure means of communication, including airwaves

Other
Facilitate the entry and exit of U.S. ships
Increase the number of employees at U.S. bases and so forth

chapter 1, it has been repeatedly argued—and accepted by the government—that even apparently noncombat operations, such as transport or supply operations, can be regarded as the use of force if they constitute an integral part of combat. It may sound easy to draw the line, but it has turned out to be extremely difficult to establish clear-cut criteria. Another legal battle arose over the geographical definition of "surrounding area," a term criticized by the opposition as being too vague and therefore dangerous. However, it was obvious that if a concrete geographical boundary was defined, it would include specific areas or countries, further complicating the debate.

And so went another battle in the war between the pacifists and the realists. However, when the law was finally enacted in the summer of 1999, many people felt that Japan had come a long way. Some analysts attributed the change in the political climate that made enactment possible to various incidents related to North Korea, including the launching of a Taepodong missile over Japan in 1998 and the repeated intrusion in Japan's territorial waters of ships, apparently from North Korea, that were suspected of carrying out some illegal mission. As Japan has seldom been exposed to threats from abroad, many Japanese tend to assume that unless Japan starts a war, the nation is immune to attack. As discussed, that is the basic assumption of the pacifists; however, once that assumption is shaken, perhaps the instinct to survive becomes stronger.

Antiterrorism Measures in the Aftermath of 9/11

The terrorist attacks in the United States on September 11, 2001, prompted further legislative measures regarding the role and mission of JSDF. From the outset, the Japanese government considered the attacks unpardonable acts of violence against not only the United States but all humankind; moreover, it was dreadful to contemplate the fact that the terrorists responsible would willingly detonate whatever weapons of mass destruction (WMD) might be available to them. European countries immediately invoked their collective right of self-defense in fighting terrorism. It would have been prudent for Japan to do likewise, but the constitution prohibited it. In order to engage the JSDF within the constitutional constraint in various support missions for the United States and other like-minded countries in fighting terrorism, a new law had to be enacted.

The Diet swiftly passed the Antiterrorism Special Measures Law in the autumn of 2001. There were some attempts by the pacifists to oppose its passage, by arguing, for example, that terrorism should not be addressed by military means but by some appropriate international tribunal, although one did not exist. However, the predominant mood among the Japanese people was one of support for the government, which argued that Japan should regard the fight against international terrorism as a challenge to itself and should extend as much support and cooperation as possible to the U.S. endeavor. The new law stipulates that to ensure that the support measures do not constitute the threat or use of force, they will not be implemented in areas where combat is taking place. The permitted support measures include supplying fuel for ships; transporting fuel by JSDF ships; transporting personnel and goods by JSDF aircraft; and providing repair, maintenance, medical, and seaport services. As of the end of 2002, two supply ships and three escort ships, including one Aegis-type destroyer, were operating in the Indian Ocean. By March 2003, these ships had carried out 213 rounds of supply operations to deliver a total of 290,000 kiloliters of fuel to U.S. Navy ships as well as to ships of the navies of other like-minded countries, such as the United Kingdom, Canada, and France. The JSDF air force also has deployed C-130 and other aircraft to carry out transport operations.

Only a decade ago, the notion of engaging the JSDF abroad had aroused fury in Japan. But photographs of JSDF ships operating in the Indian Ocean have evoked the feeling among the Japanese that Japan has come a long way, not toward the resumption of militarism, as the pacifists warned, but toward a closer working relationship with other like-minded countries in their fight against terrorism. It is a manifestation of the Japanese people's realization that in the twenty-first century it might be in Japan's national interest—as well as being, perhaps, Japan's moral obligation—to contribute actively to the international community's quest for a safer world.

The SACO Process in Okinawa

While the evolution regarding the role and mission of the JSDF overseas was under way, the military bases in Okinawa became an important item on the agenda of the U.S.-Japanese alliance. Some basic aspects of the issue are summarized below.

—*Historical background*. The Satsuma clan, which was based in Kagoshima, invaded and took control of the Ryukyu Islands in the early seventeenth century. In the late nineteenth century, the Meiji government ended the reign of the Ryukyu dynasty and established Okinawa Prefecture.

In the final phase of World War II, the battle of Okinawa—the only ground battle ever fought in Japan—took place, leaving 200,000 dead, including a huge number of civilians. After the end of the war, Okinawa was placed under the administration of U.S. forces, and during the 1950s the construction of U.S. military bases proceeded against the background of the Korean War and heightened regional tensions in Asia. Okinawa finally reverted to Japan's control in 1972.

—*Strategic importance*. The geostrategic importance of Okinawa is best illustrated by its proximity to all major cities in East Asia. It is within a 1,000-kilometer radius of Fukuoka, Taipei, and Shanghai; within a 1,500-kilometer radius of Seoul, Osaka, Hong Kong, and Manila; and within a 2,000-kilometer radius of Tokyo, Beijing, and Vladivostok. Furthermore, Okinawa is located on the final leg of the sea lane from the Indian Ocean to Japan. The bases in Okinawa, along with bases in Hawaii, Guam, and South Korea, are strategic locations for the forward deployment of U.S. forces, which play a vital role in maintaining peace and security in Asia and the Pacific region. The bases allow the prompt deployment of forces following any outbreak of hostilities.

—*U.S. bases*. As of 2001, approximately 25,000 U.S. military personnel were stationed at U.S. bases in Okinawa (army: 800; navy: 2,100; air force: 7,000; marines: 15,000); these bases constitute about 10 percent of the total area of Okinawa Prefecture. In the fall of 1995, a rape committed by U.S. military personnel stationed in Okinawa triggered outrage and an upsurge in anti-base sentiment among the people of Okinawa, who felt that they alone had had to bear the burden of hosting the U.S. bases. If the maintenance of U.S.-Japanese security ties was crucial to the national interest of Japan, why were prefectures on the mainland not prepared to share the burden by accepting U.S. bases on their own land? In response, the Special Action Committee on Okinawa (SACO) was established in the autumn of 1995. The mandate of SACO was to develop recommendations on ways to realign, consolidate, and reduce U.S. facilities and adjust the operations of U.S. forces in Okinawa to reflect the respective obligations of Japan and the United States under the security treaty.

In particular, it was decided to pursue the possibility of constructing a sea-based facility to replace Futenma Air Station, which had become the focal issue in the SACO process. However, the committee's task involved seeking solutions to satisfy inherently contradictory requirements, namely, to reduce the impact of the activities of U.S. forces on communities in Okinawa while at the same time maintaining U.S. military readiness. In view of the political reality that other prefectures are unlikely to be willing to host bases, it is difficult to envision a sweeping resolution of the base issue. Although the committee finished its mandate toward the end of 1996, it is important for the Japanese government to continue its efforts to reduce the burden on the people of Okinawa.

The U.S.-Japanese Alliance: Prospects and Options

More than half a century after the establishment of security ties between Japan and the United States, it may be worthwhile to reflect on possible new developments that may affect the basis of the ties and to propose alternative ways of dealing with them.

Twelve years after the end of the cold war, it appears that thus far the international community has failed to construct a safer, more stable, and peaceful world order. The 1990s brought a resurgence of deadly ethnic strife, notably in the Balkans, which had been frozen in many areas during the cold war. In Asia Pacific, serious flashpoints remain that require vigilant attention and persistent efforts to diffuse the tension. The Korean Peninsula, where thus far catastrophe has been averted, requires a redoubled effort to secure peace and stability in view of North Korea's admission of its renewed development of nuclear facilities. Although hopefully both sides of the Taiwan Strait are aware of the high stakes they have in averting a military showdown, a possible scenario for the eventual peaceful resolution of the issues has yet to emerge.

The political instability in Indonesia since the end of the 1990s—accompanied by threats of secession by its provinces, which could trigger the dissolution of the whole country—continues to haunt the region. And in the spring of 2002, India and Pakistan were literally on the verge of the war over Kashmir, which has been one of the most dangerous flashpoints in the world for more than half a century. A nuclear exchange there could result in a death toll of ten million, and instability on the subcontinent also could threaten the security of the vital sea lane through the Indian Ocean that connects the oil-producing Persian Gulf region and East Asia.

Moreover, the peace process in the Middle East, which had looked so promising and irreversible in the mid-1990s, has collapsed. As casualties mount in both Israel and the Palestinian territory, there seems to be no easy way to restart the peace process.

Above all, the terrorist attacks of 9/11 have totally changed the international community's perception of the threats that it faces in the new century. The realization that the perpetrators of the attacks would detonate weapons of mass destruction if they were available has forced nations to learn new rules of the game in trying to maintain international peace and security.

In reviewing possible changes in the security environment that might affect the U.S.-Japanese alliance, the following issues must be examined: first, the basic rationale of the United States for maintaining a military presence in Asia Pacific; second, specific developments in the region that can affect its security; third, possible alternatives for Japan to its alliance with the United States; and finally, the impact of the new threat of terrorism and weapons of mass destruction on the U.S.-Japanese alliance.

First, can it be assumed that the United States will continue to see maintaining a military presence in Asia Pacific as important to its national interests? As long as the United States adheres to the strategic notion that its continued presence is essential to prevent the domination of Asia through coercive means by a power that is hostile to the United States, the U.S.-Japanese alliance will remain what often is described as the linchpin of U.S. security policy in Asia and the Pacific. During the cold war, when much of Asia was under the domination of communist regimes, the United States applied a policy of containment to try to prevent the communist takeover of the remnants of the free world in Asia. It was a zero-sum game between the two blocs, at least until the U.S. rapprochement with China in the early 1970s.

Today, although serious flashpoints remain, the zero-sum game is no longer being played in Asia. Virtually all the countries in the region—with the notable exception of North Korea—attach the highest priority to achieving economic prosperity through the free flow of goods and capital in the international market system. This evolutionary change—through which the countries in the region have come to place a great deal of importance on maintaining and advancing their mutual economic interests—has had a balancing effect on the security equation in Asia. In this new setting, the nature of the U.S. presence is certainly different from what it was under the containment policy. Perhaps it can be described as a policy of keeping the options open in case some country opts for taking a hostile and disruptive approach in its dealings with its neighbors, in defiance of the deepening shared interests within the region. Because of the high cost of becoming the object of U.S. containment, no country is expected to be tempted to pursue military confrontation or dominance in the region through coercive means.

Second, how are regional flashpoints likely to affect the existing security arrangement? Obviously, a dramatic development in the Korean Peninsula or the Taiwan Strait is bound to have an impact on the way both the United States and Japan address the alliance. In both areas, the U.S. military presence in Asia Pacific has effectively deterred the outbreak of hostilities. At the time of this writing, determining how to handle the renewed challenge of nuclear development by North Korea has once again become an urgent priority not only for the United States, South Korea, and Japan, but also for many other countries in the region, notably China. The implication of this development for the security of Japan is discussed in depth in chapter 4. Suffice it here to stress that it may signal a crucial phase in the quest for peace and stability in the peninsula. Obviously, if the region's security issues were resolved in such a way that the U.S. presence was no longer required, a review of the alliance would be conducted.

In South Korea, serious debate has been under way for some time as to whether the continued presence of U.S. forces would be needed after the successful unification of the peninsula. The debate in part reflects the strong hope held by the people of South Korea for the success of President Kim Dae Jung's "sunshine policy" toward North Korea, which is discussed in detail in chapter 4. Even if unification were achieved after devastating hostilities in the peninsula, indicating the failure of the sunshine policy, the same question should be addressed. Some argue that in view of the rising nationalism among the South Koreans, which is likely to become stronger after unification, South Korea—or rather, a unified Korea—will be tempted to terminate its security ties with the United States. Others argue that the U.S. presence still would be needed as a power-balancing agent whose new function might be to deter Japan. It is interesting that in these debates in South Korea, China has not been cited as a possible justification for the continued presence of the United States; China does not seem to be perceived as a threat there. Be that as it may, any change in the security arrangement between the United States and South Korea is bound to ignite serious policy debate in Japan about future security options. However, the ways a unified Korea and Japan address their respective ties with the United States would depend on how unification is achieved. For example, if unification were achieved following hostilities in which a huge loss of human lives occurred, it would be literally impossible to predict how the national psyches of South Korea, the United States, and Japan would be affected. Under such circumstances, the extent to which China had played a cooperative and constructive role in containing hostilities and working for an early resolution of the crisis could become an important factor in deciding the future of security ties with the United States. If the prevailing perception is that China played an adversarial role during the process, the dominant mood in South Korea and Japan might support a continued U.S. military presence. Meanwhile, if the U.S. perception is that its cooperative relations with South Korea and Japan had not functioned effectively during the hostilities, the frustrated U.S. people might demand termination of the U.S. presence.

On the other hand, if unification were achieved following reconciliation of North and South Korea and the successful resolution of security issues such as the development of weapons of mass destruction, then the extremely festive atmosphere that would ensue in the unified Korea and in Japan might force a serious review of their respective security ties with the United States. However wonderful, such a scenario is too hypothetical to warrant speculation on possible policymaking at that point.

Another important factor that could affect the fate of U.S.-Japanese security ties is China's future posture. If unification were achieved peacefully, and on top of that, if the Taiwan issue were peacefully resolved and the military buildup by China did not look menacing, then domestic pressure in Japan for a complete overhaul of the security arrangement would become stronger. But again, such a scenario is too hypothetical, although pursuing it remains a crucial task for all the countries concerned. The military buildup by China is discussed in chapter 5.

Third, against the background of the new security environment at the turn of the century, it may be worthwhile to revisit various alternatives that have been advocated in Japan in the past to replace the U.S.-Japanese alliance.

Unarmed Neutrality

The option of unarmed neutrality was passionately advocated during the cold war era to avoid Japan's entanglement in any confrontation between the two blocs. Much of the rationale for neutrality has since disappeared, but what of an unarmed or substantially disarmed Japan? Because the United Nations is as unlikely in the foreseeable future as it was half a century ago to be equipped with its own forces as envisioned in Article 7 of Chapter 7 of the UN Charter, relying on the UN to guarantee Japan's security is not an option. A more likely scenario involves the formation of a multinational force by like-minded countries pursuant to a resolution of the Security Council authorizing member states to take all necessary measures to respond to a security challenge. But it does not make much sense for Japan to proceed with its substantial disarmament, thereby abandoning its ability to defend itself, and then rely on a multinational force for protection in case of armed attack. Things simply do not work that way.

Gaullism

The definition of Gaullism requires careful scrutiny. In Japan, its main features would be the termination of the U.S.-Japanese alliance and the robust buildup of defense capability following revision of Article 9 of the constitution. If Japan were to follow the logic of the original French Gaullism, it would have to think about the development of its own nuclear capability, since the termination of the alliance would mean that the U.S. nuclear umbrella would no longer be offered. However, in view of the extremely strong sentiment in Japan against nuclear weapons, developing Japan's nuclear capability is not a viable alternative. It should be pointed out, however, that if North Korea eventually becomes fully capable of launching a nuclear strike on Japan and the Japanese people believe that the U.S. nuclear umbrella may not be reliable, then advocates of Gaullism in Japan may begin to call for exercising Japan's nuclear options, which is bound to trigger nationwide controversy.

Japanese Gaullism in its purest form would be related to the belief that in order to recover Japan's full independence, it is essential to abrogate such agreements as the U.S.-Japanese security treaty and the constitution, both legacies of defeat in World War II. Although at present support seems marginal, if the Japanese people eventually were to become discontented and frustrated over the way the alliance is managed, it might increase. It should be noted that if xenophobia becomes an important issue in Japan, not only the United States but also other key players in Asia, notably China, are likely to become targets as well. In that scenario, the Gaullists might have to agonize over whether to maintain their xenophobic posture toward both the United States and China or to maintain the U.S.-Japanese alliance in order to improve Japan's strategic position in relation to China.

Obviously, the Gaullist option would not be cost free for Japan. On the contrary, the economic burden of the necessary defense buildup would be considerable. In particular, if the area around the Indian Ocean were to be destabilized by the takeover of some coastal countries by al Qaeda–type fundamentalists, protecting the sea lane without the support of the U.S. Navy would be a staggering task for the JSDF. In addition, a Gaullist foreign policy would be bound to trigger serious negative reactions from Japan's Asian neighbors as well as the United States. In the past, it often was argued that the U.S.-Japanese alliance was the cap on the bottle that prevented the genie—Japanese militarism—from getting out. Obviously, the Japanese government never espoused such an argument, because it would be outrageous for the government to accept and support the notion that unless Japan is constrained, the country might revert to militarism. Occasionally the United States used the "genie out of the bottle" argument to allay the nervousness of Japan's Asian neighbors about the U.S.-Japanese alliance. If other Asian countries shared the impression that the genie finally was free, Japan would face an entirely different security environment. It seems highly doubtful that Japan's security would be better served under such circumstances.

Regional Multilateral Framework

In the mid-1990s, the Higuchi Committee, which was entrusted with the task of studying the long-term security policy of Japan, suggested that Japan should pursue the possibility of using a multilateral framework to ensure Asian regional security. That was the period when the ASEAN Regional Forum was established, the first body to address the security agenda in the region. Since then it occasionally has been argued that efforts should be made to create in Asia some kind of multilateral organization like NATO in the post–cold war era. The underlying rationale for the multilateral approach seems to be to reduce the importance of the bilateral alliances with a view to reducing the element of confrontation in regional relations overall. Certainly, the ASEAN Regional Forum has the potential to become the key vehicle for confidence building and conflict prevention in the region, by, for example, helping to resolve territorial disputes in the South China Sea. However, the forum cannot be expected to play a decisive role in the resolution of truly precarious issues, such as tension over the Korean Peninsula or the Taiwan Strait. Although confidence-building and conflict resolution efforts might help reduce tension, they cannot substitute for an effective deterrence mechanism to prevent the outbreak of hostilities. Although NATO members' perceptions of threats to their security have greatly diminished in the post–cold war era, NATO still is an alliance based on its members' collective right of self-defense. In order to guarantee members' peace and security, any regional multilateral entity must be equipped with a collective mechanism for the use of force. Under the present circumstances in Asia, where reconciliation and reduction of tension remains the first order of business in some regions, such as the Korean Peninsula, and where shared values like those underlying NATO have yet to emerge, it seems unlikely that in the foreseeable future any such multilateral entity can be formed that includes all countries in the region.

Alliance without Bases in Japan

It is occasionally argued that, with a view to alleviating the burden on Okinawa of hosting U.S. military bases, a new security arrangement should be agreed upon, under which U.S. forces would withdraw from Japan and return only to defend the country against actual attack. However, unless the United States concludes that forward deployment of its forces no longer is essential for the maintenance of effective deterrence—thanks, perhaps, to spectacular advances in military technology—and assuming that the constitutional constraint banning the exercise of the collective right of self-defense remains, any attempt by Japan to terminate the use of bases could be construed as follows: "You should get out of Japan, because your presence is a huge nuisance. However, if we are attacked, you have to defend us. But if you are attacked, as you know, we cannot fight with you." The possibility of maintaining a viable alliance under such circumstances is questionable.

That does not mean that the burden on the local host community should be ignored. Unless local grievances are properly heeded and ongoing efforts to alleviate the burden are made, the effectiveness of the security arrangement is bound eventually to dwindle.

New Threats and the War on Terrorism

The analysis thus far has focused on the Asia Pacific region, in which Japan and the United States have a shared vital interest. The four alternatives to the current security arrangement mentioned above were conceived primarily in the context of the regional security environment. However, in the aftermath of 9/11, two fundamental goals of U.S. security policy are to fight terrorism and to reduce the number of weapons of mass destruction and prevent their proliferation. It is important to assess the ways that the alliance may be affected by the emergence of new types of threat, as well as by the U.S. global war on terrorism.

Just as the takeover of Afghanistan by the Taliban in the mid-1990s made al Qaeda's attacks on 9/11 possible, today any development in the remotest parts of the world could facilitate the spread of the global terrorist threat and the possible use of weapons of mass destruction. Terrorist cells found in Southeast Asia constitute a type of threat that had been unknown there, and the October 2002 terrorist attack in Bali was a stark manifestation of the deadly threat that terrorism poses for all the countries in the region.

No one has a clear idea of how the fight against terrorism might eventually end. The fight will be a protracted one, requiring enduring vigilance and close working relationships among like-minded countries. Still, because the threat is totally different from the familiar threats of the cold war and regional conflicts, some conceptual rethinking is needed. Simply put, the crux of the concept of deterrence is "If you harm me, I will kill you." In terms of state relations, state A is expected to refrain from attacking state B because the costs of doing so would exceed the expected gains. Deterrence depends on the rational behavior of the parties in conflict. During the cold war, the concept of mutually assured destruction, MAD, was an extreme form of deterrence for the United States and the Soviet Union.

However, deterrence may not be effective against certain types of threat. First, deterrence seems to be totally ineffective against parties such as the perpetrators of the 9/11 attacks and their followers. Unlike states, they do not occupy a fixed physical territory where damage can be inflicted on them. Moreover, although their actions were evil, their self-righteousness, based on fundamentalist religious beliefs, was more appalling. Against foes who are eager to die in order to fulfill their "sacred" mission, deterrence would not work at all.

Second, deterrence may not be effective against a so-called rogue state when it is on the verge of collapse. And because of the very "rogue" nature of the state, the possibility of its collapse is considerably higher than in an ordinary country. A case in point is Iraq. During the Operation Desert Fox bombing campaign against Iraq in December 1998, it was widely assumed in Israel that as long as the campaign was not meant to overthrow Saddam Hussein, Iraq was unlikely to launch weapons of mass destruction against Israel. However, if the life of Saddam became the primary target, deterrence against the use of such weapons would no longer be effective. In that case, the only way for Saddam to die a hero of the Arab world would be to release his remaining weapons of mass destruction against Israel.

In view of the potential ineffectiveness of deterrence, one option is to strengthen a nation's defense capability, such as its missile defense. Although it was argued in the late 1990s that missile defense might rekindle the nuclear arms race among major powers by upsetting the basis of MAD, in view of possible threats from rogue states, it has become more difficult to argue against efforts to develop an effective system, although the technical challenge is enormous. Because of uncertainty about the use of weapons of mass destruction in Asia, it would be prudent for Japan to stay in close contact with the United States on this subject.

However, as President George W. Bush indicated, a more aggressive way of addressing these threats is to take preemptive military action against terrorists and rogue states that are developing weapons of mass destruction before the weapons are actually used against other countries. Preemptive action was totally inconceivable during the cold war, when the threat of mutually assured destruction was real. It would be important, obviously, to establish some international protocol for minimizing the possibility of arbitrary preemptive action by states. In this regard, the role of the UN Security Council would be crucial. Ideally, the council would pass a resolution authorizing member states to take all necessary actions to prevent the possession of weapons of mass destruction by a specified country. However, if the council is paralyzed by the veto of any members, other members' invocation of the individual or collective right of self-defense would be inevitable.

Assuming that none of the four alternatives discussed above constitutes a viable policy orientation and that the United States regards the continuation of its alliance with Japan as vital for peace and security in Asia Pacific, the crucial question would be to what extent Japan is convinced that it would be in its own interest to maintain the alliance and work closely with the United States in pursuing its policy of global activism.

In Japan the pacifists have denounced the U.S. doctrine of preemptive action as an extreme and dangerous form of unilateralism. Many Japanese share a sense of frustration with the Europeans regarding the unilateral U.S. posture toward various multilateral undertakings, such as the Comprehensive Test Ban Treaty, the International Criminal Court, and the Kyoto Protocol. And perhaps as a result of frustrated nationalism, it has been forcefully argued that Japan should rectify the subservient posture that it has taken thus far toward the United States by adopting a more assertive and independent orientation. Such an argument may be further reinforced by the U.S. view that, given the preponderance of U.S. military power, the role of its allies is bound to be marginal. Although this U.S. view reflects in part the frustration the United States felt in conducting the Kosovo campaign with its European allies, the perception that the United States might no longer need allies could further complicate the management of its relations in Asia as well.

Certainly Japan should stress to the United States that in many respects a unilateral approach is not in the overall interest of the international community—and that in spite of its military preponderance, maintaining close working relationships with friends and allies will be indispensable in grappling with the global security challenge. One is reminded of a remark by Winston Churchill: "You can always rely on America to do the right thing, once it has exhausted the alternatives." Indeed, it can be frustrating to watch the United States exhausting alternatives. Still, the bottom line for Japan is whether its security interest would be better served by downgrading or even abrogating its alliance with the United States. It seems that in spite of the problems and shortcomings of some U.S. policies, it is still in Japan's interest to support as much as possible U.S. global activism to secure international order by fighting terrorism; preventing rogue states from possessing weapons of mass destruction; maintaining a robust deterrent capability to prevent the eruption of hostilities at various flashpoints, such as those in Asia Pacific; and continuing the quest for resolution of conflicts such as those between the Israelis and the Palestinians and between India and Pakistan. Simply put, no other country is likely to be capable of achieving those objectives. The unique strength of the United States consists not only of its military preponderance but also of what Joseph S. Nye Jr., the dean of the Kennedy School of Government at Harvard University, described as "soft power": namely, basic values such as freedom and democracy and the dynamism of its society and culture and the opportunities it offers, to which so many people all over the world are attracted.[3] "Yankee go home, but take me with you" was how

---

3. Joseph S. Nye Jr., *The Paradox of American Power: Why the World's Only Superpower Can't Go It Alone* (Oxford University Press, 2002).

the *Economist* depicted the ambivalence that many people harbor toward the United States.[4] As U.S. global activism unfolds in the coming years, certainly this sense of ambivalence will manifest itself in Japan. All sorts of reservations and criticism regarding U.S. actions will be vociferously expressed, as in the debates during the cold war. However, in the final analysis, Japan's best option seems to be to work closely with the United States, with which Japan shares not only many interests but also basic values.

4. "Present at the Creation: A Survey of America's World Role," *Economist,* June 29, 2002.

3 The Economic Relationship between Japan and the United States

Relations between Japan and the United States since the end of World War II have been dominated by security concerns, which demand the maintenance of an effective alliance, and economic concerns, which occasionally have given rise to quasi-adversarial disagreements over various trade issues. As long as the friction is confined to the affected sectors in each country, it remains an economic problem. More often than not, however, politicians in both countries mobilize to defend the interests of the affected sectors, and it becomes a political problem. When it is presented as an example of the unfairness of Japan or the high-handedness of the United States, evoking public indignation and anger, it evolves into an international problem.

Initially, the sources of friction reflected the stage of Japan's economic development, starting with textile products in the 1960s and early 1970s, followed by beef, citrus, steel, and automobiles in the late 1970s; electronics and telecommunications in the early 1980s; satellites, construction, and fighter aircraft toward the end of the 1980s;

and automobiles and auto parts, Japanese government procurement of medical and telecommunications equipment, public works, and deregulation throughout the 1990s. Eventually trade talks between the United States and Japan began to take an all-embracing approach, including efforts such as the Structural Impediment Initiative (SII), which attempted to resolve the structural aspects of the problems, and framework talks with the Clinton administration, which covered macroeconomic issues, sources of trade friction, and what was called "the common agenda."

The persistence of the trade imbalance between the two countries was the key factor in the flare-ups over trade. Aggravating the tension was the notion, which had endured in the United States since the 1970s, that various kinds of intricate Japanese regulatory measures and corporate networks such as *keiretsu* blocked the entry of foreign players into the Japanese market. The argument that the huge bilateral trade imbalance would not exist if the Japanese market were genuinely open to U.S. products had strong resonance among Americans; the very existence of the imbalance therefore was seen as undeniable evidence of unfair practices by the Japanese.

In the early 1990s, the overall picture was truly worrisome. At the time, the so-called revisionist school, led by people like Chalmers Johnson, argued that because Japan's culture and values were different, applying traditional free trade policy to Japan was ineffective and should be stopped. They considered Japan to be an emerging threat, determined to disrupt and overtake the economies of other developed countries by its "predatory" approach to trade. With the end of the cold war, the Soviet Union had ceased to be a political adversary of the United States, and there seemed to be a real danger that the vacancy would be filled by Japan, not as a political but as an economic adversary. The combination of hubris on the part of the Japanese about the strength of the Japanese economy and the faltering confidence in the early 1990s in the United States about U.S. economic strength created the worst possible setting in which to address trade friction. The first half of the 1990s was devoted to the resolution of trade issues with the Clinton administration, which attempted to take a results-oriented approach with Japan. In the second half of the decade, following the marked recovery of the U.S. economy on one hand and the prolonged recession in Japan on the other, the overall political-economic environment surrounding trade issues changed dramatically.

The Early Phases of Trade Disputes

There was a notable parallel between the trade imbalance and the intensity of trade friction. Until the end of the 1960s, the strength of the U.S. economy compared with that of the Japanese economy was overwhelming, and the United States could afford to continue to be magnanimous, accepting the aggressive penetration of its markets by Japanese goods and tolerating Japan's closed market. Moreover, the U.S. global trade deficit remained manageable. The first phase of tension over trade began when the U.S. bilateral trade deficit reached $4 billion in 1972. At the time, the export of textile products from Japan, which adversely affected the U.S. textile industry in the South, became a serious political issue. In response to U.S. government requests to rectify the imbalance, the newly installed prime minister, Kakuei Tanaka, took a series of active measures to increase Japanese imports from the United States.

There were three general types of trade friction. The first related to the penetration of the U.S. market by Japanese goods. The United States tried to deal with it by asking Japan to apply some form of export restraint, as in the case of textile products, or by imposing import-restriction measures, such as the antidumping tax, countervailing duties, and safeguards. Also included in this category was the imposition of punitive tariffs in retaliation for trade practices deemed unfair.

The second related to the difficulty of offering U.S. goods and services in the Japanese market. The United States asked Japan to open its market by lifting the ban on certain U.S. imports, notably agricultural products like rice, or at least by rectifying quotas and other import restrictions on U.S. products such as beef and citrus fruit. It also asked for changes in the regulatory system to allow access of U.S. goods and services—such as medical products and telecommunication, construction, and legal services—to the Japanese market.

The third type of trade friction related to macroeconomic policies. The macroeconomic aspects of trade often became the subject of intense negotiation, reflecting the awareness on both sides that the growing trade imbalance could not be dealt with effectively unless they were addressed as well. The agenda included, for example, the stimulation of domestic demand so that the pattern of export-led growth in the Japanese economy could be modified.

The second phase of trade friction started when the U.S. bilateral deficit began to expand again, toward the end of the 1970s. Steel and

Figure 3-1. *U.S. Trade with Japan, 1971–2000*

U.S.$ billions

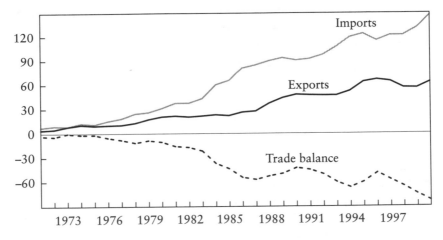

Source: U.S. Census Bureau, Foreign Trade Statistics.

automobiles, the key industrial sectors in the United States, were among the sources of friction. During the 1980 presidential election campaign, one candidate tried to convey his tough posture on the trade issue by indicating that if elected he would shut the Japanese out of the U.S. market and let them sit in their Japanese cars, munching on Japanese citrus.

As shown in figure 3-1, U.S imports from Japan started to rise spectacularly in the 1980s, ushering in the third phase of trade friction, in the mid-1980s. Tension remained high well into the 1990s. The import/export ratio reached 2.96 in 1985 and stayed at 3.06 for another two consecutive years. Japan argued that the high ratio was the outcome of U.S. macroeconomic policy, which maintained a huge budgetary deficit and a strong dollar. The U.S. had a trade deficit not only with Japan but also with practically all its major trading partners, and the overall U.S. trade imbalance with the rest of the world soared. The U.S. export/import ratio with Taiwan, Korea, and Hong Kong reached 3.3, 2.1, and 2.5 respectively in 1987. However, because of the sheer size of the bilateral deficit with Japan—which reached $56.4 billion in 1987, accounting for roughly one-third of the global deficit—Japan was the primary target of

Figure 3-2. *U.S. World Trade, 1971–2000*

U.S.$ billions

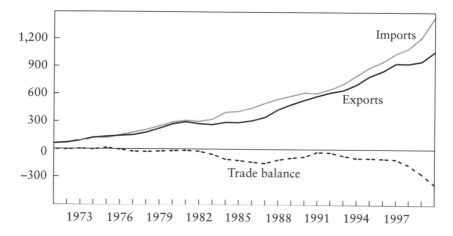

Source: U.S. Census Bureau, Foreign Trade Statistics.

U.S. anger. In 1985 the United States, once the world's largest creditor nation, became a debtor in relation to the rest of the world (figure 3-2).

Sources of friction in the third phase included semiconductors, computers, and satellites, which were the vanguard of high-tech development. Against the background of nationwide anger in the United States, the revisionists argued that the whole pattern of Japanese economic behavior—including its so-called predatory penetration of foreign markets and exclusion of foreign goods and services from its domestic market—was something bizarre, different from that of all other players in the international economic system. The perception of a uniquely Japanese threat and the notion that Japan's policies were somehow different carried dangerous connotations that could have paved the way for the introduction of import restrictions solely against Japan.

Throughout the history of trade friction between Japan and the United States, both countries were acutely aware that their tension and anger over trade could not be allowed to spill over into the realm of security or to adversely affect their alliance. Because President Ronald Reagan's top priority was to apply active pressure on the Soviets to reverse the tide of the cold war and eventually roll back communism, maintaining good relations with Japan under the leadership of Prime Minister Nakasone was important to the United States as well as Japan. However, as a quasi-adversarial atmosphere over trade began to prevail, it became increasingly challenging for both to decouple the tension in the realm of trade and the political goodwill in the security arena. Even more caution was required in dealing with trade frictions in the 1990s, when, after the end of the cold war, maintaining the alliance no longer seemed to be a paramount U.S. priority. Furthermore, with the disappearance of the Soviet Union as the primary U.S. adversary, there was a genuine danger that Japan might come to fill the position, not in political but in economic terms, in the eyes of the American public. In the United States at the time, loss of confidence in and anxiety about the future became stronger, in stark contrast to the overconfidence bordering on hubris that prevailed in Japan in the final phase of the bubble economy.

Against this background, two developments should be briefly mentioned. The first is the battle over the "Super 301" clause of the Omnibus Trade and Competitiveness Act passed by the U.S. Congress in 1988. This clause was a strengthened version of Section 301 of the Trade Act of 1974, which called for taking a tough posture toward unfair trade practices by foreign countries. Super 301 obligated the government to submit to Congress an annual report of unfair trade practices by foreign countries, decide the priority of unfair trade practices to be addressed, negotiate with the countries involved with a view to eliminating the practices, and take retaliatory measures if the negotiations were not completed within a year.

As far as the United States' other trading partners were concerned, the whole premise of Super 301 was unacceptable. A basic assumption of GATT and the World Trade Organization (WTO) is that disputes involving unfair trade practices are to be settled in accordance with the provisions of the WTO, but the United States had taken upon itself the right to judge the fairness of others. If every country were to act on its own opinion of the fairness of its trading partners, international trade would become chaotic. The Japanese government made it clear that it was not prepared to proceed with negotiations at gunpoint. It did, however, indicate its readiness to resume regular negotiations, without the threat of unilateral retaliatory measures, to seek resolution of any issue. As it happened, disputes involving supercomputers, satellites, and forest products, which were initially designated by the United States as priority items under Super 301, were resolved through routine negotiations between the two countries.

The second development, which reflected growing U.S. frustration with trying to deal with sources of friction on an individual basis, was the launching of the Structural Impediment Initiative in 1989. The SII was intended to address the structural aspects of the existing trade imbalance, and while the United States initially planned to take up only Japanese structural problems, Japan insisted that those of the United States be addressed as well. The catchphrase was "two-way talks"; each country would state its case regarding the issues under discussion. The United States proposed action by Japan in the following six areas, where it believed many problems originated:

—*Saving and investment.* The high propensity to save in Japan was the root cause of the trade imbalance.

—*Land use.* The exorbitant price of land in Japan was the cause of insufficient social infrastructure—such as well-maintained highways, parks, and other public amenities—and the Japanese people's excessive propensity to save so that they could eventually purchase a house.

—*Distribution.* The distribution system was a typical structural impediment to the entry of foreign goods into Japan.

—*Prices.* Because of the cumbersome distribution system, prices of Japanese goods on the domestic market tended to be much higher than prices of Japanese exports, in total disregard of Japanese consumers' interests.

—*Exclusive trade practices.* Entry into the Japanese market by new-comers, including foreign companies, was extremely difficult.

—*Keiretsu.* Keiretsu, a practice whereby major companies maintained long-term working relationships with a network of specific other companies, also hampered the entry of newcomers.

Japan proposed action by the United States in the following seven areas:

—*Saving and investment.* Insufficient saving in the United States was the root cause of the imbalance.

—*Investment and productivity.* Investment to increase productivity was essential for enhancing U.S. international competitiveness.

—*Business practices.* To become more competitive, U.S. businesses should rectify their short-sighted practices.

—*Government regulation.* U.S. regulations often hampered international trade.

—*Research and development.* Research and development were essential to international competitiveness.

—*Export promotion.*

—*Labor force training.*

What seems remarkable in looking at these items fourteen years later is the premise of the Japanese argument. In essence, Japan was saying that an overall improvement in the performance of the U.S. economy was badly needed to rectify the imbalance. Given that since then the world has witnessed both the impressive performance of the U.S. economy and the deplorable stagnation of the Japanese economy, one cannot help wondering what prompts the rise and fall of national economies.

In the end, the SII produced the following actions by Japan:

—Public investment amounting to ¥43 trillion over ten years

—Measures to facilitate the opening of large foreign retail stores, such as Toys R Us, to help improve the distribution system

—Strengthening of the functions of the Fair Trade Commission to deal more effectively with exclusive trade practices.

Actions taken by the United States included the following:

—Measures to tackle the budget deficit stipulated in the president's budget message of 1990

—Acceptance of the importance of taking a longer-term perspective in order to improve the competitiveness of U.S. businesses

—Various programs for labor force development.

Meanwhile, however, despite some breakthroughs in changing trade regimes and systems in Japan, U.S. frustration over disappointing outcomes led to stronger support for taking a so-called results-oriented approach to trade. In past negotiations, the basic aim of both parties had always been to seek a compromise on trade regimes and mechanisms—for example, by lifting some restrictions or deregulating a certain sector. However, in a market economy, no government can possibly guarantee the end results of such measures, such as a certain quantitative increase in trade in the sector involved. The semiconductor arrangement of 1986—a compromise in which the two countries maintained totally different positions on the basics—is a case in point. The United States insisted that Japan commit itself to securing a certain share of the Japanese market for the sale of U.S. semiconductors. Japan refused on the grounds that its economy was not centrally controlled and that it was, as a matter of principle, impossible for the government to secure a market share for any product. This was the first clash over the results-oriented approach. It was resolved through a somewhat opaque arrangement in which Japan expressed its official view of the future prospects of the market share for U.S. semiconductors by stating, in essence, that the Japanese government recognized that the United States expected the share of sales by foreign companies in the Japanese semiconductor market to exceed 20 percent in five years. A new statement, agreed upon in 1991, contained basically the same language, with a slight elaboration: "This expectation is realizable. The Japanese government welcomes the fulfillment of this expectation. Both governments are agreed that the above description does not constitute the guarantee of market share."

The statement was presented as something like a weather forecast. Who would claim that a weather forecast creates a binding obligation on the meteorologist who delivers it? The United States, however, had a different interpretation of the nature of the arrangement: the Japanese government was obliged to make every effort to help achieve the target, and if the actual share turned out to be too far short of the target, Japan might be subject to some retaliation. Although the arrangement was the outcome of a bona fide effort by both parties to avoid a split over the issue, it established a precedent for the U.S. pursuit of the results-oriented approach.

The Fourth Phase

The fourth phase of trade friction between Japan and the United States was Japan's dispute with the Clinton administration. As the famous one-liner of the 1992 Clinton campaign, "It's economy, stupid!" succinctly indicated, the incoming administration's paramount priority was the recovery of the U.S. economy. U.S. economic statistics for 1991 were pretty gloomy. GDP growth was –0.5 percent, while the unemployment rate was 6.8 percent, rising to 7.5 percent in 1992. The overall trade deficit amounted to $66.7 billion, of which the deficit with Japan was 65 percent. Japan still seemed to be in good shape, with GDP growth of 3.8 percent, an unemployment rate of 2.2 percent, and the current surplus-to-GDP ratio steady at 3.0. Because the United States no longer maintained a perpetual trade surplus with the EU, the U.S. view was that only Japan had come out a winner in the game of international trade, amassing a huge surplus, and that as a result the U.S. economy remained stagnant, with increasing unemployment. Against this background, it appeared that at the outset the Clinton administration had certain basic perceptions about the Japanese economic equation: First, Japan had unique systems and customs ("Japan is the outlier of the G-7 countries" is the expression that the United States often used). Second, Japan had achieved spectacular success through its systems and customs and was unlikely to modify them voluntarily. Third, because Japan's commitment to ensuring the transparency and fairness of its systems and procedures had not succeeded in rectifying the existing imbalance between the two countries, the emphasis should be placed not on the improvement of systems and procedures but on obtaining Japan's commitment to achieving certain future results. Fourth, exerting pressure on Japan was effective; the Super 301 clause, in particular, should be actively applied.

In the summer of 1993, another round of comprehensive economic talks between the two countries, the "framework talks," began (see box below).

The Framework Talks

—Sector and structural talks and negotiations

Government procurement: medical technology, telecommunications, computers, supercomputers, satellites

Deregulation and competitiveness: financial services, insurance

Other important sectors: automobiles and parts

Economic harmonization: investment, intellectual property

Existing arrangements: plate glass, paper, forest products

—Macroeconomics (midterm objectives)

Japan: meaningful reduction of the current surplus, expanded market access, sustainable economic growth led by domestic demand

United States: considerable reduction of the budget deficit, encouragement of domestic saving, increase in international competitiveness

—Common agenda based on a global perspective

Environment, technology, labor force development, population growth, HIV, narcotics trafficking

The common agenda recognized that there were numerous areas in which the two countries could cooperate for their mutual benefit. It was meant to dispel any suggestion that dispute resolution based on a zero-sum approach to trade was the essence of the economic relationship between Japan and the United States.

At the outset, it was agreed that the talks should be of a two-way nature, that is, they should not become a forum for one-sided demands by the United States; that the results should apply to third countries on a MFN (most-favored-nation) basis; that the talks should be confined to those areas in which the government controlled the decisionmaking process; that issues should be resolved in accordance with international regulations, such as GATT; and that numerical targets should not be adopted.

Nevertheless, looking back, one gets the impression that the talks could be described as "the battle of numerical targets." At the outset, the United States insisted on the adoption of numerical targets for macroeconomic goals, such as a 1 to 2 percent reduction in the ratio of Japan's current surplus to GDP and around a .33 percent increase in the ratio of Japan's import of manufactured goods to GDP. When Japan opposed such macroeconomic targets, the United States began a vigorous attempt to introduce numerical targets in sector talks, notably in regard to government procurement and to automobiles and auto parts. Japan persisted in pointing out that numerical targets and managed trade were utterly incompatible with the basic principles of open markets and free trade.

Numerical targets related to government procurements were the most hotly debated. The United States insisted that the Japanese government's procurement of foreign products should increase by 30 percent annually for telecommunications and 25 percent for medical equipment. The basic assumption was that since the government was directly in charge of procurement, it should have some control over who supplied the items. Japan, however, rebutted that assumption; even in the realm of government procurement, the open tender with full transparency had become the norm, and the government could not take affirmative action, so to speak, in favor of U.S. products. The negotiations lasted more than a year, with a temporary suspension due to differences over the issue. In the end, the United States withdrew its demand for numerical targets and instead set up a mechanism for reviewing progress in the procurement of foreign products by the Japanese government.

Negotiations over automobiles and auto parts involved three issues—numerical targets, government control, and MFN status; the sequence of the negotiations was as follows:

At the outset, in 1993, the United States proposed that Japan should commit itself to maintaining a 20 percent annual increase in the purchase of U.S. auto parts, as in the past; that in purchasing parts, Japanese automakers in the United States should maintain the same ratio of locally produced parts to foreign parts as the big three U.S. automakers; and that the number of auto dealers in Japan that sell U.S. cars should be increased annually by a specified percentage.

In early 1994, there was a summit meeting between President Clinton and Prime Minister Morihiro Hosokawa. However, they could not reach agreement on many of the issues of the framework talks, and a cooling-off period ensued. In May 1994, the talks resumed, centering on three items: deregulation regarding spare parts; expansion of dealer networks in Japan; and Japanese automakers' voluntary program for purchasing parts manufactured by foreign companies. The gap between the two parties could not be bridged. The talks were again suspended, following the launching of an investigation into the issue by the U.S. government pursuant to Super 301.

Talks resumed in January 1995, with the understanding that voluntary purchase (VP) would not be a subject of the talks; that deregulatory measures regarding spare parts would be outside the purview of Super 301; and that negotiations regarding the purchase of spare parts would be limited to measures to improve the environment for both U.S. and Japanese businesses. All of these understandings related to distinguishing between situations in which the government can legitimately take charge and those in which it cannot interfere.

In May 1995 the United States announced the imposition of a 100 percent tariff, pursuant to Super 301, on Japanese luxury cars in retaliation against trade barriers in the auto parts market in Japan. In response, Japan initiated consultations within the World Trade Organization, pursuant to Article 22 of GATT. On June 28, 1995, two days before expiration of the time limit for negotiations under Super 301, the two parties reached the following agreement: First, within the context of the framework talks, the governments agreed on measures to increase the access of foreign car manufacturers to the Japanese market and specified various deregulation measures to be taken by the Japanese government, such as deregulation of the process of certifying repair shops, which the United

States hoped would expand sales opportunities for foreign spare parts. Second, outside the framework talks, three joint announcements were made regarding the purchase of spare parts and the expansion of dealerships; key portions are summarized below.

U.S. trade representative Michael Kantor estimated on the basis of his analysis of individual Japanese company plans that the companies' purchase of U.S. parts would increase by $6.75 billion and that their production of Japanese vehicles in the United States would increase from 2.1 million to 2.65 million by 1998. He also estimated an increase by 1998 of $6 billion in the companies' purchase of foreign parts for use in Japan.

Ryutaro Hashimoto, minister of international trade and industry, responded that the government of Japan had had no involvement in arriving at those estimates because it was beyond the government's scope and responsibility and that the estimates of the Office of the United States Trade Representative were solely its own.

The U.S. government stated its expectation that the combination of implementing the measures under the automotive framework and the intensified efforts of U.S. vehicle manufacturers would lead to a significant increase in sales opportunities for U.S. manufacturers in Japan. Specifically, the government envisioned an increase in the number of direct franchise agreements between U.S. vehicle manufacturers and Japanese dealers that would result in approximately 200 new sales outlets by the end of 1996, increasing to a total of approximately 1,000 new outlets by the end of 2000.

Again, Minister Hashimoto stated that the government of Japan had had no involvement in producing that forecast because it was beyond the government's scope and responsibility, and that the forecast was solely that of the U.S. government.

Trade representative Kantor's estimates about the purchase of spare parts were based on forecasts that Japanese automakers had prepared and then shared with the United States, but the forecasts were not a binding commitment on the automakers. Thus, the issue of numerical targets was resolved by the adoption of forecasts, from which the Japanese government effectively dissociated itself. The resolution of this issue was different from that of semiconductors in 1986 and 1991 in that the dissociation was made unequivocal. The issue of government control also was carefully sorted out so that the Japanese government was not held responsible for anything that was beyond its scope. As to the MFN issue, since the EU had become increasingly worried that Japan might make concessions only to the United States, in contravention of the MFN principle, both U.S. and Japanese negotiators were highly aware that any measures they agreed to had to be applied across the board.

The entry into force of a new agreement among members of the WTO in January 1995 altered the rules of the game as far as Super 301 was concerned. The new agreement stipulated that should the United States unilaterally impose retaliatory measures without completing the WTO dispute resolution process, the action would be defined as a clear-cut violation of the agreement. As a result, it became possible for Japan and the United States to resolve any disputes in the multilateral arena, instead of engaging in the bilateral negotiations that had often put a great deal of strain on both governments

In hindsight, the mid-1990s were a turning point for the economies of the two countries. The U.S. economy started to show robust growth in the first half of the 1990s. U.S. labor productivity in the manufacturing sector recorded annual growth of 5.1 percent from 1996 to 2001, far surpassing the growth rate of 2.7 percent in the 1970s. The strength of the U.S. economy became the key feature of the global economy, dramatically restoring the American public's confidence in and optimism about the future. Moreover, as economic stagnation continued in Japan, the perception of Japan as an economic threat faded. During this period, the structure of the U.S. global trade deficit changed. During the 1990s, Japan's share of total U.S. imports declined markedly, from 18.1 percent in 1990 to 11.1 percent in 2001, while China's share increased, from 3.1 percent in 1991 to 9.0 percent in 2001. China overtook Japan in terms of its share of the U.S. trade deficit, which in 2001 reached $83 billion, the equivalent of 20.2 percent of the total deficit. The U.S. deficit with Japan for that year was $69 billion. Because of all these changes, the emotional furor that characterized U.S.-Japanese trade disputes until the early 1990s markedly subsided.

It is interesting to note that there has not been noticeable political tension in the United States in regard to its growing trade deficit with China, unlike with Japan. That difference can be explained by three factors: first, U.S. confidence in the strength of the U.S. economy remains solid; second, much of China's exports to the United States consists of goods produced by U.S. companies in China; third, partly because of the second factor, the growing U.S. trade deficit with China does not look threatening as far as the economic equation is concerned. All three factors constitute a marked contrast to U.S. trade relations with Japan in the 1980s.

Pattern of Dispute Resolution

A typical dispute resolution scenario involving U.S. difficulty in gaining access to the Japanese market can be mildly caricatured as follows:

In the United States, a representative of some company or sector approaches Congress and the administration and forcefully argues that its attempt to enter the Japanese market has been hampered by inscrutable regulatory regimes designed to protect domestic players. Concerned senators and representatives begin to mobilize.

The United States government raises the issue with the Japanese government, and talks begin. In its opening gambit, the United States stresses that the huge trade imbalance between the two countries has come to be symbolic of the closed nature of the Japanese market, and that without a satisfactory resolution of the issue, it will become increasingly difficult for the administration to resist the rising tide of protectionism in Congress. The United States then lays its demands on the table. (Toward the end of the 1980s, Super 301 became the central theme, and the Clinton administration's insistence on numerical targets became the key issue.)

Japan responds that there is nothing wrong with the Japanese regulatory system and that in no way is Japan prepared to change it. (In some cases, such as agricultural products, Japan stresses that in view of political sensitivities or the importance of preserving said sector, U.S. demands cannot be accommodated.) Japan rebuts the argument that the trade imbalance is the result of its unfair regulatory practices or the so-called closed nature of the Japanese market. (With Super 301, Japan fiercely pronounced negotiation under gunpoint to be unacceptable and persisted in pointing out that setting numerical targets was impossible because of the very nature of a market economy.)

The Japanese media, meanwhile, take up the dispute and play up the familiar image of a merciless United States applying unbearable pressure on Japan. The U.S. media play up the familiar image of an unfair Japan jealously guarding its market against the United States.

Depending on the political value of the sector in question, members of the Diet become actively involved in preparing the Japanese negotiating position. When it becomes evident that talks at the government agency level cannot produce a solution, interaction at the top political levels, including, for example, direct communication between president and prime minister, is pursued. Eventually, both sides start searching for some sort of compromise that each finds politically palatable enough to swallow.

Once a compromise is reached, the U.S. administration starts to play it up as the best result obtainable under the circumstances and one that will prevent a further upsurge of protectionism in Congress. Meanwhile, the Japanese government stresses to the domestic audience that although it was difficult to accept, the compromise is the best option available in view of the overall importance of U.S.-Japanese relations. Depending on the nature of the compromise, the government also pledges to take every measure needed to alleviate the damage to the affected sector.

Clearly all these friction issues tended to be perceived in terms of a zero-sum game in which any compromise was bound to encroach at least to some degree on the vested interests of the two countries. As far as the people in the affected sectors were concerned, it often was an agonizing defeat. However, it should also be noted that a compromise that promoted deregulation in various sectors was often in the overall interest of the Japanese people, and in that respect not quite a zero-sum game. That point was persistently stressed by the United States during the SII talks. However, the U.S. effort in the early 1990s to force Japan to commit itself to numerical targets cannot possibly be presented as an effort to rectify the existing Japanese system in the interest of the Japanese people. Furthermore, U.S. threats of possible retaliation pursuant to Super 301 were perceived as evidence of high-handedness toward Japan.

Possible Options?

Each trade friction issue has its unique features, often embodying the long history of the sector in question. It may not make much sense, therefore, to reflect on possible alternatives and options without a detailed analysis of each sector. However, since each issue was settled through some degree of concession by Japan—by agreeing to reduce protection for some sector, notably agriculture, or by opening some segment of the Japanese market to foreign players, thereby doing some damage to domestic players—the image persisted among the Japanese people that Japan always succumbed to U.S. pressure. The people in the affected sector naturally grumbled that they were sacrificed to maintain U.S.-Japanese relations. So it may be worthwhile to reflect on whether the whole process could have been avoided by some alternative approach.

One option was to say "no" to the United States, perhaps not always, but with considerably more frequency. Saying no would require Japan to be prepared to plunge into what might be called a trade war with the United States. In response, the inevitable U.S. reaction would be not only retaliation as provided for in Super 301, but also adoption by Congress of more sweeping protectionist measures against Japan. To what extent the Japanese economy could sustain a substantial reduction in its access to the U.S. market was a serious concern. It has been argued that the U.S. economy had come to rely so much on imported goods and services that closing the U.S. market to imports, including Japanese imports, would not have been a viable option. However, it would have been a daunting exercise for Japan to gauge whether it would have been more painful for Japan to suffer reduced access to the U.S. market or for the United States to bear reduced imports from Japan. Certainly up to that point Japan had refrained from bluffing. The bottom line for Japan has been that emotionalism arising from friction over trade must not undermine the U.S.-Japanese alliance. Although the United States and the EU have engaged in some degree of trade war with each other on a number of occasions in the past, the Atlantic Alliance has not been decisively undermined; it can be argued, therefore, that a credible alliance of nations is feasible despite disagreements over trade. However, there was no persistent trade imbalance between the United States and the EU, and the perception of unfairness—the key emotional feature of U.S.-Japanese trade disputes—did not surface, in spite of a substantial clash of interests, for example, in trade in agriculture. In view of the intense furor in the United States in the 1980s over trade relations with Japan, it is doubtful that a trade war would have been handled in a cool-headed manner. However, these days the Japanese perception that Japan never said no to the United States in such disputes is taking a political toll in Japan in the form of frustrated nationalism, discussed in chapter 1.

One can argue that Japan should have said no to the semiconductor arrangements of 1986 and 1991. Although the Japanese maintained that the arrangements were nothing but forecasts that in no way constituted a binding commitment, there remained some room for the United States to insist that they represented a de facto acceptance of numerical targets by Japan. The United States considered the semiconductor arrangements to be wonderful achievements, to be emulated in subsequent negotiations. The central question was always to what extent Japan should compromise when a matter of principle is at stake. In the case of the semiconductor negotiations in the mid-1980s, Japan, against the background of emotional upheaval surrounding the dispute, judged that the format of the 1986 arrangement was the best solution.

In the case of the framework talks in 1994 about government procurement, the Japanese government could have given preference to U.S.

goods and services. It could be argued that if profound damage to the friendship between the two countries could be averted by government purchase of U.S. products, it would be worthwhile, even though it would, to a certain degree, contravene the rules related to open and transparent tender. However, throughout the talks, Japan was determined not to take too flexible or lenient a position on matters of principle. As described, Japan managed to reach agreement without doing so, and no noticeable damage was done to the bilateral relationship overall.

Another option was active recourse to the multilateral dispute resolution procedure under GATT. As mentioned, after the new WTO agreement entered into force in 1995, the United States was required to complete the WTO dispute settlement procedure before imposing retaliatory measures on another country. However, even before 1995, Japan could have taken more active and frequent recourse to the dispute settlement procedure of GATT instead of attempting to seek solutions strictly on a bilateral basis. One of the reasons why Japan was reluctant to do so was that in cases of trade disputes related to the protection of certain sectors, such as agriculture, a binding third-party verdict sounded far more ominous and unmanageable than a resolution through bilateral negotiations with the United States. However, over time, the focus of trade disputes shifted from the protection of various sectors to issues that hinged on matters of principle, which are more amenable to resolution through multilateral procedures.

Japan also could have taken a more proactive and preemptive position on the structural reform of the Japanese economy. In order for Japan to get out of its decade-long economic stagnation, the bold and determined implementation of structural reforms is essential. The fact is that the increased competitiveness and deregulation observed in various sectors as a result of U.S. demands have enhanced the overall efficiency of the Japanese economy. Japan could have carried out those measures voluntarily. If it had, the frustration arising from the perception that Japan always succumbs to U.S. pressure could have been avoided. It should be pointed out, however, that in certain cases the United States was not especially excited with the Japanese government's unilateral and voluntary measures for structural reforms, simply because they could not be presented as the result of painstaking efforts by the United States. Still, looking back on the long history of the economic relationship between Japan and the United States, one cannot help wondering to what extent Japan's protection of various sectors and its regulatory quagmire would have persisted had it not been for its trade disputes with the United States.

4 Endgame on the Korean Peninsula

North Korea's stunning admission in 2002 of its past abduction of many innocent Japanese and its clandestine development of nuclear weapons reminded the Japanese people of the stark reality that the divided Korean Peninsula remains a serious challenge to the security of Japan. In view of their anger and anguish over the abductions and their sense of betrayal over the development of nuclear weapons, it is natural that not many Japanese are convinced of the wisdom of engagement with North Korea. The gut feeling of many Japanese seems to be that there is little point in beginning a dialogue with what appears to be an utterly untrustworthy state.

The historical entanglement of Japan and the Korean Peninsula, which has extended over two millennia, culminated in the colonization of the peninsula by Japan from 1910 to 1945. Because of the two nations' history and geographical proximity, developments on the Korean Peninsula always touch a raw nerve in Japan. In that, the Korean issue is unique in Japanese foreign policy.

At present one gets the impression that Japan has drifted back to square one, where it found itself in the early 1990s.

No one can be certain of North Korea's current motives or strategies, or the assumptions on which it bases its decisions. There is a possibility that North Korea is trying to reach out in some bizarre way to the rest of the world, notably to the United States for a guarantee of survival and to Japan for massive economic assistance. Once again, the stakes for South Korea, the United States, and Japan in maintaining their solidarity are very high. It also is important to enlist the active involvement of China and Russia, inasmuch as both countries share a serious interest in maintaining a nuclear-free peninsula. For Japan, it is essential to approach this new phase of its relations with the Korean Peninsula with vigilance, farsightedness, and firmness.

Historical Background before World War II

Interaction between Japan and the Korean Peninsula, which lie near each other across the Sea of Japan, has been ongoing since prehistoric times. Waves of emigrants from the peninsula came to Japan during Japan's formative phase, around the fifth century, spreading their cultural heritage throughout the country. Because of their geographical proximity, upheaval in one country often had a huge impact on the fate of the other. During the attempted Mongolian invasion of Japan in the twelfth century, the only attempt at invasion of Japan by a foreign power, the peninsula was used by the Mongolian expeditionary force as a springboard to launch a landing operation, which was utterly devastated by a typhoon. The extremely timely arrival of the typhoon is deeply embedded in the Japanese national memory as "kamikaze" (the wind of God). Whenever an unexpectedly fortunate turn of events occurs, it is called kamikaze. (It was tragic that seven centuries later, suicide missions by Japanese military aircraft against U.S. battleships also were called kamikaze, embodying the hope of the military that the tide of the war would be reversed.)

In the sixteenth century, Toyotomi Hideyoshi, who became Japan's leader by winning a series of battles against numerous rivals, tried to conquer the peninsula. Although the memory of this abortive invasion has faded among the Japanese, it lives on in the Korean national psyche. During the Edo era (1603–1868), when Japan was tightly closed to the rest of the world, the Kingdom of Korea and the Netherlands were the only countries that maintained official contact with the Edo shogunate. The Kingdom of Korea periodically sent an official delegation consisting of selected members of the Korean cultural elite to Japan. These encounters were much appreciated by their Japanese counterparts, as they opened a rare window on the rest of Asia.

As soon as Japan launched its modernization efforts after the Meiji Restoration in 1868, the Meiji government began to intervene in the Korean Peninsula. A serious policy dispute erupted within the nascent government over whether Japan should urge the Kingdom of Korea, by force if necessary, to open itself to the rest of the world, as Japan had done only a few years before. The hardliners lost the battle when high-ranking officials who had been sent abroad came back to Japan in time to argue that compared with the Western powers that were actively engaged in the imperialistic game in Asia, Japan had insufficient military strength to embark on a venture against its neighbor. Two decades later, the clash between Japan and China about their respective influence over the Kingdom of Korea triggered the 1894 Sino-Japanese War, and Imperial Russia's attempt to expand its sphere of influence over Manchuria and the Korean Peninsula led to the Russo-Japanese War in 1904. Japan was the victor in both instances. In 1910, the Japanese government annexed the Kingdom of Korea; thus the peninsula became the first object of Japan's fateful expansion into mainland Asia.

More than half a century after the end of Japanese colonization, it remains a thorny issue between Japan and South Korea. Some Japanese historians hold the view that Japan's imperialistic expansion toward mainland Asia in the Meiji era was the inevitable outcome of its modernization efforts and that the tragic turning point in modern Japanese history was the rising tide of militarism in the 1930s that led Japan into World War II. As far as the Korean view of history is concerned, the humiliation inflicted by Japan began at the beginning of the Meiji era.

A Rough Outline of Events since 1945

During the final weeks of World War II, the Korean Peninsula was divided into two parts. The northern half was placed under the control of the Soviet Union, and the southern half under the control of the United States. In 1948, the Republic of Korea (ROK) was established in the south and the Democratic People's Republic of Korea (DPRK) was established in the north. In the summer of 1950, Kim Il Sung launched a full-scale invasion of South Korea, with the goal of unifying the peninsula. For a long time, the question of which side actually started the war was a point of contention between realists and leftists in Japan. The leftists adhered to the view that the south had started the war. For that matter, when a number of tunnels apparently constructed by North Korea were found along the 38th parallel, the leftists expressed the firm conviction that they had actually been constructed by South Korea. Such was the divisive political atmosphere in Japan during the cold war. It was primarily Russian archives opened after the end of the cold war that finally established that North Korea started the war.

By the time the armistice ending the Korean War was signed in 1953, the total numbers of those killed or wounded were estimated at 900,000 Chinese, 520,000 North Korean, and 400,000 UN troops, about two-thirds of whom were South Korean. U.S. war dead amounted to 36,000. More than half a century after the war began, legally speaking it still has not ended. What the belligerents produced in 1953 was not a peace treaty but an armistice that was signed by the commander of the U.S. forces, who at the same time signed for the commander of the UN forces; by the commander of the North Korean forces; and by the commander of China's voluntary forces. This legal structure made it possible for North Korea to insist later that the only interlocutor that it was ready to deal with was the United States, not South Korea. That was not a mere legalism but, as far as the North was concerned, the very basis of its legitimacy. North Korea argued that it was morally bound to liberate South Korea, which was ruled by a puppet of the United States, and thereby fulfill the unfinished task of unifying the peninsula. The military intervention of the United States hampered its accomplishment of that goal, and North Korea's top priority since then has been to achieve the withdrawal of U.S. forces from South Korea.

During the cold war, all the major powers—the United States, the Soviet Union, and China—were aware that the outbreak of another war in the Korean Peninsula could ignite a third world war; therefore, they dealt with the peninsula cautiously. In a sense, the cold war ensured the status quo. South and North Korea competed against each other to improve their relative standing in the international community, with the full backing of their respective allies.

In 1965, after long and difficult negotiations, Japan normalized relations with the ROK. President Park Chung Hee opted for normalization in spite of strong anti-Japan sentiment among the people of South Korea. Normalization legally ended Japan's colonization of the southern half of the peninsula, and Japan pledged economic assistance amounting to half a billion dollars over ten years to settle claims arising from that period.

Because of persistent military confrontations between North and South Korea following the end of the Korean War, it was impossible to seek a similar settlement with North Korea. Predictably, the opposition in Japan denounced normalization as a dangerous ploy to support the dictatorial military regime of the South. The argument was reminiscent of the clash over the San Francisco Peace Treaty on whether to negotiate a comprehensive peace settlement that included the Soviet Union or to accept a settlement with the United States first. In a sense, the debate over the peninsula reflected the schism between the pacifists and the realists. In spite of the opposition at home, the realists (the LDP government) staunchly supported the regime in the South. In South Korea, the strong anti-Japan sentiment that was the legacy of colonization persisted, making relations between the countries sensitive and challenging in spite of their basically shared security interests. Kim Dae Jung, who was elected president of the ROK in 1997, climaxing his long and spectacular political career, played the leading role in overcoming the history issue between the two countries, although his abduction in 1973 in Tokyo by intelligence agents of the Park government had complicated relations between Japan and the ROK throughout much of the 1970s and 1980s.

During the cold war, South Korea's dynamic economic growth steadily strengthened its international position in relation to the North. In particular, the Olympic Games held in Seoul in 1988 amply impressed on the whole world the changing power equation between South and North Korea.

North Korea and Weapons of Mass Destruction

As the cold war began to wind down, a number of developments on the Korean Peninsula altered the status quo. The Soviet Union abandoned the role of security guarantor and economic benefactor of North Korea and in 1990 normalized relations with the South, with which it hoped to develop strong economic ties. As a result, the North could no longer rely on Soviet military and economic assistance, which had been so generous during the cold war. After this rupture, it became evident that the Soviets could no longer be expected to play the crucial deterrent role they had played during the cold war if North Korea took destabilizing actions in the peninsula. In 1992, China also normalized its relations with the ROK, paving the way for the membership of both South and North Korea in the UN. Inasmuch as the North was strongly opposed to the de facto acceptance by the international community of two Koreas, normalization by the Soviet Union and China of their relations with South Korea was a huge setback. Furthermore, the economic deterioration in North Korea accelerated in the post–cold war era, in part because economic assistance from former allies was no longer readily available but also because the government had always attached the highest priority to military spending. A sense of anxiety was shared and expressed in various quarters about the possible further destabilization of the situation in the event that Kim Jong Il succeeded his father, Kim Il Sung.

The crisis regarding nuclear development by North Korea was the dominant issue in the first half of the 1990s, while in the second half, concerns over North Korea's possible acquisition of weapons of mass destruction, including not only nuclear weapons but also missiles, became the focus of attention. Those concerns were aptly addressed in the Perry report on U.S. policy toward North Korea in 1999.[1]

It seems safe to conclude that North Korea already had started a program for the eventual production of nuclear weapons back in the 1980s. Perhaps because the Soviets no longer guaranteed the country's security and its isolation in the international community was increasing, North Korea decided that it had to accelerate its nuclear program to ensure its own survival. As the Perry report pointed out, the possession of weapons of mass destruction by North Korea could disrupt the precarious balance of power in the peninsula, increasing the possibility of another war. Moreover, the prospect of the possession of nuclear weapons by a regime that might collapse in the near future was extremely worrisome, because deterrence might have no effect on a regime that is on the verge of collapse. The threat "Play nicely, or you will perish" is unlikely to have the desired effect on someone who is about to perish anyway.

In addition, in view of the past pattern of arms exports by North Korea, it was feared that nuclear weapons might become a readily exportable commodity destined for another precarious region, the Middle East. The issue, therefore, had not only regional but also global dimensions. And because of the high stakes involved, as Don Oberdorfer pointed out in his book, North Korea found itself in a position to use the issue in bargaining with the rest of the world.[2] Given North Korea's

1. William J. Perry, *Report on United States Policy toward North Korea: Findings and Recommendations* (U.S. Department of State, Office of the North Korea Policy Coordinator, 1999).
2. Don Oberdorfer, *The Two Koreas*, rev. ed. (Basic Books, 2002).

admission of its clandestine development of nuclear weapons, it is quite likely that there will be a replay of this bargaining ploy.

In 1994, the tension in the Korean Peninsula heightened as North Korea refused to accept inspection by the International Atomic Energy Agency (IAEA) and threatened to begin processing spent nuclear fuel. The UN Security Council prepared to impose economic sanctions on North Korea, and North Korea made it clear that the action would lead to war. However, as a result of a visit by former president Jimmy Carter to North Korea, an agreement was negotiated, diffusing the tension. Basically, the agreement called for providing North Korea with a light-water reactor in exchange for not only shutting down the existing nuclear plutonium reactor but also canceling the construction of much larger plutonium reactors that could theoretically generate enough plutonium to produce fifty to 100 nuclear bombs a year by the end of the decade. From the beginning, the scheme was criticized as being a reward for blackmail, namely North Korea's threat to continue developing nuclear weapons. At the time, the continued operation of the existing reactor, which already might have produced plutonium sufficient for two or three bombs, was worrisome enough, but the prospect of an unfettered North Korea producing up to 100 nuclear bombs a year was truly alarming. What else could have been done under the circumstances? That question seems to haunt us again today.

In the event, in the mid-1990s, KEDO (Korean Peninsula Energy Development Organization) was founded jointly by the United States, the Republic of Korea, and Japan to implement the light-water project, and it became an important forum for engaging North Korea. The ROK agreed to bear roughly three-quarters of the construction costs of the reactor, while Japan expressed its readiness to contribute roughly U.S.$1 billion. Initially it was argued that by the time the project was completed, the peninsula would be united, and therefore the project would not entail a loss of money for the ROK. It is not clear whether that argument had any impact on the ROK's decisionmaking.

In the latter part of the 1990s, it became clear that North Korea was vigorously pursuing the development of long-range missiles. In 1998, North Korea conducted a test launch of a Taepodong missile over Japan, igniting serious alarm among the Japanese. The Perry report advocated a two-pronged approach: if North Korea demonstrated readiness to give up its development of weapons of mass destruction, then the United States and its allies would prepare to take positive steps to improve their respective relations with the North; if, on the other hand, North Korea persisted along its provocative path, they would take steps to ensure their security and contain the threat. The report was the outcome of close consultation among the three key allies: the United States, the Republic of Korea, and Japan. In fact, the most commendable achievement with regard to the security of the peninsula in the 1990s was the close consultation and cooperation among the three countries in grappling with the newly emerging challenges of WMD development by North Korea. Before that, there had been no such endeavor among the three, partly because the security situation was more predictable during the cold war and because the political climate in both Japan and the ROK was not ripe for such a close tripartite working relationship.

Meanwhile, President Kim Dae Jung, who was inaugurated in 1998, began to pursue his so-called sunshine policy. The gist of the policy seemed to be peaceful coexistence between North and South Korea and the eventual reconciliation of the two through increased interaction and cooperation, which would, in essence, take the form of various financial flows from the South to the North. In June 2000, the historic North-South Summit between Kim Jong Il and Kim Dae Jung was held in Pyongyang, apparently ushering in a promising new era for the Korean Peninsula. However, throughout 2002, a sense of impasse prevailed, although attempts were made to move forward with reconciliation, for example, by connecting railway lines across the 38th parallel. Toward the end of the year, North Korea, perhaps emboldened by the election in the South of Roh Moo Hyun, who pledged to continue the sunshine policy, stepped up its brinkmanship regarding the resumption of plutonium processing in Yongbyong.

Normalization of Relations between Japan and North Korea

It was evidently the Soviet Union's decision to normalize relations with South Korea that prompted North Korea to propose normalizing relations with Japan in the autumn of 1990. Like the normalization of Japan's relations with South Korea in 1965, normalization of relations with the North would require Japan to settle all claims from the colonization era. That meant the eventual transfer of a considerable amount of financial resources from Japan to North Korea. At the time, fear was expressed in various quarters in South Korea that such a transfer might strengthen the military capability of the North and thereby disrupt the existing precarious military balance between North and South Korea to the disadvantage of the South. As far as Japan was concerned, although normalizing its relations with North Korea was the last remnant of postwar business that it needed to settle, it clearly was not in the security interests of Japan to disrupt that balance and destabilize the Korean Peninsula. Japan's basic goal, therefore, has been to complete normalization in such a way as to contribute to the peninsula's peace and stability. However, in part because of North Korea's refusal to address squarely the issue of its abduction of Japanese citizens in the 1970s and 1980s, no progress was achieved throughout the 1990s.

The Abduction Issue

The abductions were a truly outrageous, unforgivable, and perhaps unprecedented state crime. Naturally Kim Jong Il's stunning admission to Prime Minister Koizumi in September 2002 of the abduction of many innocent Japanese nationals by North Korean operatives and the disclosure that many of them had died prematurely triggered an unprecedented wave of anguish and anger among the Japanese people.

The abduction issue has several unique features. First, the abduction of innocent foreign nationals by a state agent—and the possible killing of some of them—could be regarded as casus belli under traditional international law. Because it could lead to war, and because the perpetrating state is likely to be severely condemned by the international community, such crimes have seldom been committed.

Second, if two states maintained diplomatic relations, it would be possible at least for the offended state to convey through diplomatic channels not only its protest but also potential retaliatory measures, in the strongest possible terms. In the case of Japan and North Korea, since diplomatic relations have yet to be normalized and the basic posture of the North has been one of open hostility toward Japan, it has been extremely difficult to set up official channels of communication through which the issue could be pressed.

Third, because of the very nature of the crime, whenever Japan had a chance to take up the abduction issue with North Korea, the latter flatly refused to admit that there had been any abductions. During normalization talks in 1992, for example, the North Korean delegation simply quit the table when the Japanese delegation pressed the issue. It was much easier to push for the release of two Japanese fishermen who were set free in 1990 after having been held prisoner in the North on espionage charges since the mid-1980s, because the North at least acknowledged their arrest. Although the charges were debatable, the fishermen were not abducted, so North Korea did not have to admit to having committed a state crime in order to resolve the issue. In the event, the fishermen were released following the dispatch of a high-level, bipartisan parliamentary mission to North Korea in the autumn of 1990, headed by Shin Kanemaru, one of the most influential leaders in the LDP, and the adoption of a joint declaration on that occasion expressing Japan's readiness to compensate for its past relations with North Korea.

Finally, although such a state crime constitutes casus belli, military retaliation obviously was out of the question for Japan, and Japan had no other way to force North Korea to admit its transgression. It therefore was assumed that Japan's only option was to engage and perhaps entice the North in such a way that it would realize that resolving the abduction issue was in its own interest. That, in fact, is what happened during Koizumi's encounter with Kim Jong Il.

Humanitarian Aid

In 1995, the first time that North Korea showed any willingness to ask for help from Japan, Japan made 200,000 tons of rice available as humanitarian assistance. North Korea appeared at the time to have dropped its theretofore self-reliant posture, instead asking for assistance from the international community in a forthright way. Japan decided to help for the obvious humanitarian reasons—the food shortage in the North seemed to be worsening—but it also hoped that the assistance would help warm somewhat its existing chilly relations with North Korea so that an impasse in negotiations could be averted. In the late 1990s, as massive starvation in the North was being reported in the outside world, the Republic of Korea and the United States began to provide a considerable amount of food assistance in response to a plea from North Korea.

The critics of food assistance argued that the food shortage in the North was caused not by any natural disaster but by the government's policy of spending its economic resources on the military sector and totally neglecting productive sectors like agriculture. They argued that giving assistance under such circumstances was tantamount to subsidizing North Korea's military, which could mount lethal attacks on the Republic of Korea, the United States, and Japan in the event of hostilities.

Even though humanitarian disaster looked imminent, it was difficult to decide to what extent the strategic aspects of the issue should be given priority. On the other hand, it was argued that food assistance could serve a strategic interest as well, because it would reduce the possibility of a major upheaval in the North triggered by the deteriorating food supply and of ensuing chaos in the peninsula. It would be safer to avoid such an event if at all possible.

Security Issues

Meanwhile, three developments aggravated the negative feeling in Japan toward North Korea: the testing of a Taepodong missile over Japan in 1998; frequent intrusions into Japan's territorial waters by armed ships suspected of having been sent from North Korea for hostile missions, one of which was scuttled after a battle with a pursuing Japanese patrol boat in 2002; and the growing frustration among the Japanese about the impasse over the abduction issue. The Taepodong test affected three issues. First, because of the strong sense of frustration among many Japanese politicians and media that Japan had to rely entirely on photographs taken by a U.S. reconnaissance satellite in monitoring developments in the Sea of Japan, the government decided to begin to develop its own satellite. Second, the political climate became much more receptive to the notion of missile defense, to be studied jointly with the United States. Third, the test created a favorable political climate for passage of the law related to the role of the Japanese Self-Defense Force in developments in the area surrounding Japan, discussed in chapter 2.

In 2000 the Japanese government decided to give another half-million tons of rice to North Korea despite growing anti–North Korea sentiment in Japan. It was hoped that dialogue with North Korea would be resumed so that these pending issues could be pressed. In the event, the impasse continued.

Defining Parameters and Options for the Peninsula

North Korea's abrupt introduction of various economic reforms in the summer of 2002, which suggested that it might have decided to try the market mechanism to revitalize it economy, and its stunning admission of the state crime of abduction and of ongoing development of nuclear weapons call for reconsidering the key parameters of the quagmire in the

Korean Peninsula. What sorts of policy options are available for Japan, the Republic of Korea, the United States, and two other key players, China and Russia, to avert catastrophe and reduce tension?

The core issue appears to be the nature of the regime in North Korea and its ability to survive. At the outset, the very concept of President Kim Dae Jung's sunshine policy aroused strong suspicion and hostility in the North, where the eventual collapse of the regime was believed to be the policy's ultimate objective. Whether to dismantle the regime with a strong dose of sunshine or by freezing it out was only a question of tactics; the strategic objective remained the same. Such was North Korea's original, and perhaps still latent, suspicion.

It is obvious that in order to resolve its chronic economic difficulties— in the worst years, thousands of people died of starvation—the North must change its entire system, in line perhaps with what Deng Xiaoping began in China in the early 1980s under the banner of "Reform and Opening." Simply put, it seems essential for the North to adopt a functioning market economy in which the free initiative of its citizens is valued; to hook the national economy to the international economic system, ensuring the free flow of goods and capital; and finally, to shift available resources, including the labor force, away from the military sector to the productive sectors, such as manufacturing and agriculture. The conventional wisdom among North Korea watchers, however, suggests that those are precisely the changes that North Korea's leaders, afraid of triggering the collapse of the regime, are least willing to make. What they seemed to be prepared to tolerate was a limited opening in which the inflow of potentially destabilizing information from the outside world could be minimized. Instead of reducing the military sector, the North Korean leadership seemed determined to maintain the military capacity needed to ensure the survival of the regime in the face of possible instability caused by the increasing influx of what was in their eyes toxic information from South Korea and the rest of the world. They appeared to be deeply worried that South Korea and the United States would take advantage of any such instability to attempt to overthrow the regime.

Since the mid-1990s, North Korea has been trying to create and maintain what can be described as a MAD (mutually assured destruction) approach to North-South relations by means of conventional weapons. The concept of MAD originated during the cold war, when a nuclear strike by either side would have resulted in the annihilation of all mankind. In the Korean Peninsula, limited MAD is ensured not by nuclear but by conventional weapons—an arrangement that is somewhat unique in the world today. In effect, North Korea has taken Seoul hostage. If war erupted, Seoul could be totally devastated in the first few days by a deadly barrage of artillery from North Korean positions amassed along the 38th parallel. One often gets the impression that, after all, South Korea may not be too worried about North Korea's acquisition of nuclear weapons and missiles simply because the North does not need them to inflict horrific damage on the South. Evidently, the massive use of conventional weapons would suffice. Perhaps this MAD approach prompted President Kim Dae Jung to conclude that the only way to avert possible catastrophe was to firmly establish a state of peaceful coexistence between North and South through the sunshine policy. The crucial assumption of the sunshine policy seemed to be that if South Korea and the United States assured North Korea that they were not working toward the collapse of the regime—and instead were prepared to guarantee its survival—then North Korea would be relieved of its paranoia about its own survival and eventually would cease to be a threat to the security of South Korea and the rest of the world. On the basis of that assumption, the South expressed its readiness to make huge economic benefits available to the North, with a view to impressing on the North its genuine desire for reconciliation. However, an extremely important question remains: to what extent is such benevolence linked to reciprocal action by the North regarding key security issues, such as the exercise of credible restraint on the development of weapons of mass destruction and the reduction of the conventional arms amassed along the 38th parallel? As far as South Korea is concerned, a logical corollary of the sunshine policy might be that as long as peaceful coexistence is firmly established, reconciliation is achieved, and the North's distrust is allayed by the guarantee of survival given by the rest of the world, then whatever weapons the North might possess is of secondary importance. These days it seems that many South Koreans have come to assume that invasion by the North is unlikely; in fact, this perception of the disappearance of the North Korean threat may be one of the key reasons why presidential candidate Roh Moo Hyun overwhelmed his rival, Lee Hoi Chang, who asserted that the sunshine policy was a failure and that a tough stance should be taken against North Korea. Many people in South Korea appear to feel that since invasion by North Korea is unlikely, there is no need to make such a fuss about its development of nuclear weapons or missiles.

However, this view differs markedly from that of the United States, especially in the aftermath of the September 11 terrorist attacks. The U.S. position is that al Qaeda–type terrorists are eager to obtain weapons of mass destruction and that the "axis of evil" countries, including North Korea, are developing weapons of mass destruction and might assist terrorists in acquiring them. Since that would threaten the security not only of the United States and its allies but also of all mankind, it is unlikely that the United States would accept the notion that as long as peaceful coexistence is established in the Korean Peninsula, North Korea's possession of weapons of mass destruction can be tolerated.

In the course of dialogue and contacts between the United States and North Korea throughout the 1990s, the North persisted in its effort to obtain a guarantee of survival from the United States, for the obvious reason that only the United States has the military capacity to obliterate the North. To the North, a guarantee of survival from the South is totally inadequate. The Clinton administration seemed ready to give its guarantee as long as North Korea would give up its WMD capability. One wonders what would have happened if Clinton had had an additional six months in office in which to conclude missile talks and make a presidential visit to Pyongyang. In view of North Korea's revelation of its continued development of nuclear weapons, perhaps the most likely course of events would have been temporary excitement followed by eventual impasse. It is very doubtful that Kim Jong Il would have abandoned his quest to ensure his survival by maintaining his MAD policy in exchange for some limited improvement in his relations with the United States.

As for Japan, needless to say, the possession of nuclear weapons by North Korea would be a truly nightmarish and totally unacceptable development. It is suspected that North Korea might be eager to develop another MAD strategy in regard to Japan, through the combined threat of nuclear weapons and Nodong missiles, so that it has the luxury of holding two hostages, South Korea and Japan, to ensure its survival. North Korea may believe that although the United States could eventually win a war in the Korean Peninsula, before it could claim victory, North Korea would have inflicted unbearable damage on South Korea and Japan, with an enormous number of dead and wounded. The North Korean regime's possession of the military capacity to inflict such damage is logically the only guarantee it has of its own survival. Meanwhile, in Japan the pacifists may believe that no one needs to worry about such a doomsday scenario because unless the United States or South Korea initiates a military venture against the North, there will be no catastrophe in the first place. Japan, then, should work with South Korea to help establish a state of peaceful coexistence in the peninsula—the prerequisite being a guarantee of survival for North Korea.

During the cold war the annihilation of the human race was fortunately averted because both sides in the conflict realized that since neither could win a nuclear war, peaceful coexistence was their only option. That was what MAD was all about. However, the situation in the Korean Peninsula is entirely different. As the Perry report indicated, North Korea's possession of weapons of mass destruction would mean a serious risk of war in the peninsula. What makes a rogue state distinctively dangerous is the persistence of several risks:

—The domestic situation can veer dangerously out of control, and under such circumstances deterrence no longer works against the regime, which faces impending collapse.

—The regime tends to resort to brinkmanship in order to grab whatever concessions it can from other states, and the risk of mistaking a real threat for a bluff—and thereby precipitating a real catastrophe—can be high. Today in particular, as North Korea threatens to resume the production of plutonium, one cannot help wondering what future rounds of brinkmanship would bring if the North is finally equipped with nuclear capability.

—There always remains the possibility of collusion between terrorists and the rogue state.

What are the options for the key players? First, North Korea's admission of its clandestine development of nuclear weapons puts the United States in a quandary in terms of the consistency of its policies toward North Korea and Iraq. Since the United States argued in defending its invasion of Iraq in March 2003 that the preemptive use of force was necessary to prevent Saddam Hussein from using the weapons of mass destruction that it accused him of having, the obvious question is whether the United States is bound to eventually make a preemptive strike against North Korea, whose threat to develop nuclear weapons seems more ominous than any threat from Iraq. And what about regime change? If the United States considered regime change in Iraq essential to eliminate any future threats from Saddam Hussein, how about North Korea? In view of North Korea's past pattern of destabilizing behavior and severe human rights violations, one might naturally conclude that, just as in Iraq, regime change in the North is a prerequisite for peace and stability.

Or the question might be asked in the context of the Munich Agreement, which was intended to halt Adolf Hitler's aggression. If the lesson of Munich was that the United States and like-minded countries should not appease Saddam Hussein, what of appeasing North Korea? Answers to these questions depend, of course, on whether war can be considered a viable option in the Korean Peninsula. Because of the MAD policy between North and South Korea, war in the peninsula would result in massive casualties, with a death toll of perhaps one million, including not only soldiers but also a huge number of civilians. Thousands of war dead might be inevitable among the U.S. forces stationed in South Korea as well. The war against Iraq entailed no such prospect of overwhelming numbers of dead and wounded. It is understandable, then, that the United States has indicated its preference for resolving problems with North Korea through diplomatic means. The doctrine of the preemptive strike may have to be modified so that its use depends on a kind of cost-benefit analysis, the cost being the magnitude of casualties that the United States and its allies would be expected to suffer and the benefit being the eradication of the threat from weapons of mass destruction and avoidance of possible future casualties among U.S. and allied forces.

The Bush administration apparently has never felt comfortable with the notion of engagement with North Korea. It has shown strong repugnance toward the 1994 Agreed Framework between the United States and North Korea, which it considers the appeasement of an outlaw. If, however, in 2003 as in 1994, the basic assumption is that the military option cannot be pursued, then theoretically at least three options suggest themselves.

The first option is to refuse to talk with North Korea and simply ignore it, the rationale being that the United States should not succumb to intimidation. As a result of its subsequent isolation in the international community, North Korea would be expected to back away from the brink. The risk of this option, however, is that it may end up as de facto acquiescence to North Korea's development of nuclear weapons. North Korea might continue to raise the level of brinkmanship and, in total defiance of its isolation, begin to produce enough plutonium to produce several nuclear bombs within a matter of months.

The second option is more or less a replay of the events of the first half of 1994, that is, to impose economic sanctions against the North. One difference between 1994 and 2003 may be that whereas in 1994 it was assumed that a resolution of the Security Council was needed to impose sanctions, in 2003 a UN resolution may not be needed. Key countries, notably the United States and Japan, can tighten the screws on North Korea through unilateral measures, such as suspending financial transfers from Japan and preventing illegal actions by North Korean ships. Since 1994, North Korea has become much more dependent on humanitarian assistance to cover its food shortages. Furthermore, owing to the bankruptcy of quasi-banking institutions in Japan that used to supply substantial amounts of funds to the North, it can be assumed that North Korea's cash revenues have been sharply reduced. Compared with 1994, therefore, today sanctions should be more effective. However, North Korea may refuse to be intimidated by the threat or imposition of sanctions and continue the game of brinkmanship by starting to produce plutonium.

The third option is to try to work out a "grand bargain" with North Korea. This option would require highly coordinated action among the United States, the Republic of Korea, and Japan. Evidently North Korea continues to hope to obtain a guarantee of survival by using the development of weapons of mass destruction as a negotiating card. After all, it has no other card to play. However, the United States would feel considerable reluctance to give any such assurance, which would obligate it to support the regime if an internal attempt was made to topple it from power, and the notion of supporting such a coercive, totalitarian government is unlikely to be popular with the American people. What the United States could offer instead is a commitment not to make a preemptive attack against North Korea as long as the North gives up all military capability, nuclear and conventional, needed to maintain its policy of mutually assured destruction. Its disarmament would, of course, have to be thoroughly verified. Obviously, even if North Korea agreed to forgo developing weapons of mass destruction and to reduce its conventional arms along the 38th parallel, working out a truly effective arrangement for inspection and verification, which it would be highly likely to resist, would be extremely difficult. Perhaps it would entail more rounds of brinkmanship, since North Korea might very well interpret U.S. attempts to enforce inspections as a ploy to destabilize and trigger the collapse of the regime.

Japan already has resumed dialogue with North Korea, in the form of continued normalization talks. Japan's basic position is very simple. Normalization of relations and provision of economic assistance to settle past claims with the North will be impossible unless the following conditions are met:

—The abduction issue is fully resolved—with thorough disclosure by North Korea, return of the family members of the abducted people to Japan, prosecution of the actual perpetrators, and compensation to Japan for the state crime.

—North Korea immediately ceases to develop nuclear weapons.

—North Korea ceases all other aggressive behavior, such as sending armed ships into Japanese territorial waters for illegal missions.

In short, normalization of relations cannot occur unless North Korea is genuinely ready to work for peace and stability in the peninsula. Predictably, the North's response was that the abduction issue already had been resolved and that the nuclear issue was none of Japan's business and should be settled between the United States and North Korea. Therein lies an important prospect for close coordination between the United States and Japan. The United States can stress that if North Korea is prepared to accept the dismantling of its weapons of mass destruction, to be carried out under a thorough inspection scheme; to remove its forces from the 38th parallel so that the threat to Seoul is substantially reduced; and to resolve the abduction issue, then it can expect not only the United States' guarantee of no preemptive strikes—alleviating the regime's obsession with its survival—but also a massive infusion of economic assistance from Japan. There may be psychological resistance among decisionmakers in the United States to the idea of offering North Korea a reward for abandoning actions that it should not have taken in the first place, and their reservations regarding its behavior are likely to be much more profound since its disclosure of clandestine nuclear activities. The question of trust is likely to have considerable resonance everywhere, including Japan.

Needless to say, the role of the Republic of Korea is the key factor in the entire endeavor. It has been truly worrisome to watch the recent upsurge of anti-American feeling in South Korea, which was sparked by the tragic deaths of two schoolgirls killed by an American armored vehicle on a training exercise in June 2002. When the two American soldiers involved eventually were acquitted by a U.S. Army court, the South Koreans' fury increased. However, even before the accident, there was growing sentiment among South Korean youth that the U.S. military presence was an obstacle to peace and the eventual unification of the peninsula. In contrast to the older generation, which still remembers that the United States saved the South during the Korean War and effectively guaranteed its security thereafter, the majority of the younger generation may no longer be convinced that South Korea needs a guarantee of security from the United States. It is remarkable and somewhat ironic that following the democratization and economic revival of South Korea, which the nation can be truly proud of, many younger people in the South have come to have a sense of affinity with the North, where the system of government embodies the last remnants of Stalinism, with concentration camps and the mass starvation of its citizens.

The worst-case scenario for South Korea, the United States, and Japan (which North Korea might consider its best-case scenario) is as follows:

Anti-American feeling further escalates and becomes politically uncontrollable in the South, as a majority of South Koreans become convinced that a U.S. security commitment no longer is needed. The tough posture of the United States toward the North on weapons of mass destruction is regarded in the South as an arrogant U.S. ploy to prevent peace and reconciliation between North and South. Many in the South claim that, after all, North Korea's weapons of mass destruction are aimed only at Japan and the United States and therefore do not constitute a serious threat to South Korea.

In response to such anti-American outbursts, domestic sentiment in the United States toward security ties with South Korea rapidly deteriorates. Americans find it utterly incomprehensible that the South does not understand the grave concerns that the United States has about weapons of mass destruction, but if the majority of South Koreans do not want a guarantee of security from the United States, they reason, what is the point of maintaining a military presence there? Perhaps if the United States withdrew its troops, it would have a freer hand in terms of military options. Furthermore, there is bound to be a serious rupture between Japan and South Korea in terms of national interests if it becomes evident that North Korea possesses nuclear weapons and the South remains untroubled by it and continues to transfer generous quantities of economic resources to the North. At that point it will become crucial for the United States to reaffirm the credibility of the nuclear umbrella extended to Japan. Otherwise, Japan could face an agonizing choice between accepting the position of easy victim of nuclear blackmail or developing its own nuclear capacity, which could trigger internal turmoil in Japan.

It is to be hoped that the key leaders of the three countries fully appreciate their huge stakes in averting such a scenario, inasmuch as all three nations would lose if it were realized. Former president Kim Dae Jung seems to be fully aware of the gravity of the game of brinkmanship and the possible emergence of a nuclear-armed North Korea. The first meeting between President Bush and the newly installed president, Roh Moo Hyun, is hoped to have foreclosed the possibility of such scenario.

From the standpoint of Japan's security, of the three options discussed, the first, de facto acquiescence to North Korea's possession of nuclear weapons, is utterly unacceptable. The second option, applying economic sanctions, would be acceptable if it forced North Korea to give up its nuclear development activities and acquiesce to other demands. However, if it failed to have the desired effect, the North still may eventually develop nuclear weapons. Option three, the grand bargain, seems to be the inevitable choice, as long as war is not the fourth option. It can be argued that option three does not, after all, reward North Korea's aggression, because in exchange for a guarantee of no preemptive strikes and for possible economic assistance, the North must drastically change its orientation, by giving up weapons of mass destruction, curtailing its capacity to destroy South Korea with conventional arms, and accepting intrusive inspection and verification procedures to ensure its compliance with the first two conditions. In essence, North Korea is expected to give up the very capabilities that its leadership believes essential to its survival, and to commit itself to becoming a normal, civilized member of the international community. It is quite possible that the North would consider the rewards offered for changing its behavior inadequate. Even if the Republic of Korea, the United States, and Japan eventually agree to try option three, it is bound to be an extremely difficult and frustrating endeavor.

The Republic of Korea would support wholeheartedly the notion that the nuclear issue should be resolved through negotiation; after all, it is bound to suffer most if war breaks out. However, it must forgo any notion that as long as reconciliation and peaceful coexistence can be achieved, the resolution of the WMD issue can be postponed. Besides, a scenario in which the two Koreas bask in the sunshine together, leaving the United States and Japan in the shadows, seems unlikely in view of the fact that as far as North Korea is concerned, peaceful coexistence is meaningless unless the United States guarantees its survival, and its quest for economic rehabilitation is infeasible without economic assistance from Japan.

As mentioned, all three options are based on the assumption that option four, the use of force—or, to be more precise, preemptive attack—by the United States is not a viable option because of the huge risks involved. It should be noted, however, that totally eliminating the possibility of preemptive attack would quite likely embolden North Korea in its familiar practice of brinkmanship. It therefore seems important to maintain some degree of ambiguity about the possibility of preemptive attack. If both option two and option three were tried and failed to produce desirable outcomes and North Korea engaged in further rounds of brinkmanship involving nuclear weapons, an argument in favor of option four might surface.

In any endeavor to work out a grand bargain, the support of two key players, China and Russia, must be enlisted. During the previous crisis in 1994, China seemed to be genuinely worried about the prospect of a nuclear-armed North Korea. In the present circumstances, China might insist that it does not have much influence on the North. Still, the stakes for China are extremely high. The prospect of a massive inflow of refugees from North Korea must be a nightmare. If a grand bargain can be worked out and the Korean Peninsula stabilized, it would obviously be in China's strategic interest as well. Evidently the influence of Russia on North Korea is considerably weaker than was that of the Soviet Union during the cold war. Nevertheless, as a country that was crucially involved in the strategic game in the peninsula for a long time, Russia could be expected to make a valuable contribution to the endeavor.

Before closing, it should be stressed that Japan must continue its efforts to further improve its relations with the Republic of Korea. In spite of the two nations' shared security interest, deepening economic interdependence, and common values of freedom and democracy, their contemporary relations often have been complicated by the past. The defining occasion was the memorable official visit to Japan of President Kim Dae Jung in 1998. He expressed his readiness to close the history issue by making, in essence, three points: that the history issue is one that Koreans will never be able to forget; that nevertheless, they are aware that the Japanese, having learned the lessons of history, have changed; and that Korea appreciates the economic cooperation that Japan has generously extended to it in the past. In response, Prime Minister Keizo Obuchi expressed his heartfelt remorse and apology for the fact that Japan had caused tremendous damage and suffering to the people of the Republic of

Korea during the colonization period. Since then, there has been a marked surge of friendly feeling toward the ROK among the Japanese people. It is extremely encouraging to note that the World Cup, which was jointly hosted by Japan and the Republic of Korea in 2002, has further solidified relations between the two countries. However, it should not be assumed that this awakening of friendship between the two countries will continue and flourish automatically. On the contrary, each must make conscious and hopefully dynamic efforts to cement these positive developments, which are a tremendous asset to both.

5 Relations between Japan and China

Thirty years after the normalization of relations between Japan and China, the polarization among the Japanese regarding Japan's policy toward China has become conspicuous. The percentage of those expressing unfavorable views of China has increased markedly since the 1970s and 1980s. According to an opinion poll conducted annually by the Japanese government to gauge the degree of friendly feeling among the Japanese people toward foreign countries, the percentage of those responding that they had positive feelings toward China reached its highest point, 79 percent, in 1980 (figure 5-1). In the same year, 15 percent reported unfriendly feelings. Much the same pattern continued through 1988. In 1989, because of the Chinese government's suppression of protest at Tiananmen Square in Bejing, in which hundreds of demonstrators were killed, the friendliness percentage dropped to around 50 percent, while the unfriendliness percentage exceeded 40 percent. In 1996, perhaps owing to military exercises that China conducted in the Taiwan Strait earlier that year, the percentage of those reporting unfriendly feelings reached 51 percent, overtaking the friendliness percentage,

Figure 5-1. *Japanese Attitudes toward China, 1978–97*

Percent

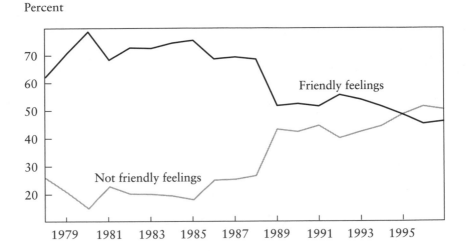

Friendly feelings

Not friendly feelings

1979   1981   1983   1985   1987   1989   1991   1993   1995

Source: "Public Opinion Poll on Foreign Policy," Office of Public Information, Cabinet Office of the Japanese government, February 4, 2002.

which dropped to 45 percent. While Japanese direct investment in China has resumed and is now at its most robust since the turn of the twenty-first century, it is vociferously argued that Japan should discontinue ODA (Official Development Assistance) for China. ODA was made available at the end of the 1970s, when Deng Xiaoping called for a radical change in China's basic policy orientation, from the pursuit of ideological purity to the pursuit of economic development. Obviously, how China proceeds down the path to modernization will have an enormous impact not only on East Asia but the whole world in the twenty-first century. It therefore is extremely important for Japan to reflect once again, thoroughly and rationally, on the options for forming its policy toward China, since managing their mutual relations is likely to be the most challenging task Japan will face for at least the next couple of decades.

A Rough Historical Sketch

The early normalization of Japan's relations with the People's Republic of China (PRC) was not pursued because of the security ties between Japan and the United States. Prime Minister Shigeru Yoshida was not fully convinced of the wisdom of the rigorous containment policy of the United States in the 1950s, and the loss of access to China, which had been a supplier of natural resources as well as a crucial market in the prewar era, was considered a serious handicap for the economic reconstruction of Japan. However, those were the days when a Chinese volunteer force prevented UN forces under the leadership of the United States from claiming victory in the Korean War, which could have resulted in the unification of the peninsula by South Korea. It also is probable that without the U.S. defense commitment, Taiwan would have been taken over by the PRC. Because normalization of relations with China would surely have wrecked U.S.-Japanese relations and because of Chiang Kai-shek's generous posture toward Japan regarding a postwar settlement, Prime Minister Yoshida opted for establishing formal relations with the Republic of China in Taiwan. In an attempt to maintain economic ties with the mainland, the government adopted a policy of the so-called separation of politics and economics. However, since the PRC was bogged down in domestic turmoil over various matters, such as the Great Leap Forward program in the late 1950s—which was intended to increase industrial and agricultural production but ended in terrible disaster and the Cultural Revolution in the 1960s, economic transactions with the PRC did not give a massive boost to Japan's economic reconstruction efforts, contrary to original expectations.

Against a background of rapprochement between China and the United States in 1971, as well as of growing support within the LDP for normalization of relations with China, normalization was achieved under Prime Minister Kakuei Tanaka in 1972. In their joint statement, the Japanese government recognized the government of the People's Republic of China as the only legitimate government of China; the government of the People's Republic of China reiterated its position that Taiwan was an indivisible part of the territory of the PRC, and the Japanese government said that it fully understood and respected that position; and the government of the People's Republic of China renounced its claims against Japan for war reparations.

As a result, Japan terminated its official relations with Taiwan, and a joint entity was to be set up to look after the countries' nongovernmental relations. Compared with normalization between the United States and China in 1979, the task was a little simpler in that, unlike the United States, Japan did not have defense relations with Taiwan. On the other hand, Taiwan had been a colony of Japan until the end of World War II. Because of this historical legacy, Beijing had been all the more sensitive about the relations between Japan and Taiwan, although Japan had renounced all rights and claims to Taiwan in the San Francisco Peace Treaty.

It took another six years to conclude the Peace and Friendship Treaty between Japan and China, owing to the difficulty of handling the antihegemony clause, which stated that neither party would seek hegemony in the Asia Pacific region or any other region and that both would oppose any such attempt by any other state. China strongly insisted that the clause be included in the treaty, but "antihegemony" was considered a euphemism for "anti-Soviet," and Japan was reluctant to accept the straightforward inclusion of the clause for fear of unnecessarily provoking the Soviet Union. In the event, a compromise was reached in which the treaty was to include both the antihegemony clause and a clause clarifying that the treaty did not affect the position of either country with respect to their relations with other countries. The fact that the Chinese were adamant about the antihegemony clause, as a kind of litmus test of anti-Soviet sentiment, testified to the complexity of the Asian power equation in the 1970s.

Deng Xiaoping's new policy orientation, which, under the banner of modernization, attached the highest national priority to economic development, ushered in a new era in China as well as in relations between China and Japan. To what extent Deng was prepared at the outset to tolerate the erosion of socialism by introducing a market economy is unclear. Still, the shift from the pursuit of ideological purity to the pursuit of economic development through the market thirty years after the communist revolution was truly a spectacular change. Also notable was China's new readiness to accept foreign loans and investment. Up to that point, any notion of dependence on foreigners was anathema to China's basic economic philosophy of self-sufficiency. Toward the end of the 1970s, China expressed readiness to accept direct loans from the Japanese government on concessionary terms to finance various projects in key sectors of the Chinese economy. This marked a fundamental change in relations between Japan and China. Throughout much of the 1970s, the possibility that one day China would willingly accept assistance from Japan looked extremely remote, as China was bogged down in the final phases of the power struggle between the ideologues, such as the Gang of Four, and the realists, led by Deng. Deng's new market orientation was favorably received by the Japanese people, who perhaps had never felt comfortable with China's earlier revolutionary zeal. The new orientation, however, was one with which the Japanese were quite familiar, and, as noted, friendly feeling among the Japanese toward China reached its highest point, 79 percent, in 1980. Throughout the 1980s, it looked as though China's political system also was headed toward a certain degree of democratization. However, after the student movement was crushed in Tiananmen Square, it became apparent that any move toward democratization in China was to be deferred. Although after the Tiananmen incident, Japan, in solidarity with the other G-7 nations, had imposed sanctions on China, Japan was the first country to lift sanctions and worked to help China out of its international isolation. Although the Japanese were appalled by the brutality of the incident, there was noticeable hesitation to take measures that might decisively wreck relations with China, but human rights became a thorny issue in the 1990s. Whenever Japan raised the issue, China's standard rebuttal was that it was an internal affair in which foreign countries were not entitled to intervene; that what was most urgently needed to improve human rights in China was the elimination of poverty; and that because of its past atrocities, Japan was in no position to raise the issue of human rights in China. Thus the emotional link between the human rights issue and the history issue became a unique feature of the relations between Japan and China.

Challenges in the 1990s and Afterward

Chinese economic development accelerated markedly in the 1990s. In the first half of the decade, China recorded double-digit growth every year, and over the entire decade, its trade with the rest of the world more than quadrupled. Trade between Japan and China showed an almost fivefold increase during the same period. There was an upsurge in Japanese direct investment in the Chinese manufacturing sector in the early 1990s, followed by a lull in investment in the late 1990s, when the perception was widespread among Japanese businesses that investment in China might not be as profitable as it was once assumed to be. However, since 2001, there has been a resurgence of Japanese investment, perhaps spurred by the prospect of China's accession to the World Trade Organization. A notable feature of the 1990s is that foreign investment acted as the main engine of China's trade expansion. Toward the end of the decade, roughly half of both its exports and its imports were conducted by foreign companies operating in China.

In 1992, Deng made a clear-cut pronouncement regarding the legitimacy of China's new policy orientation, declaring that as long as the expansion of productivity, strengthening of the national economy, and improvement in the standard of living could be achieved under a certain system, that system could be called socialism. Thus Deng in effect accepted the legitimacy of the capitalist approach, dispelling any remaining hesitation among conservatives. Deng's policy has been faithfully followed by his successor, Jiang Zemin, so much so that in 2001, private entrepreneurs—that is, capitalists—were allowed to join the Communist Party. More than half a century after the end of the revolution, China has truly come a long way.

The 1990s were a defining period for China in terms of the nation's active participation in the global economy; today, China is one of the key players. By 2001 China's international trade was the sixth-largest in the world, and over the next several years it will become the fourth largest, after that of the United States, of Germany, and of Japan. Globalization also has had a profound impact on the whole socioeconomic fabric in China, and on the aspirations of the Chinese people. Especially notable has been the exponential expansion of communication through the Internet and by mobile phone.

Meanwhile, in Taiwan, there was an upsurge in nationalism throughout the 1990s, as the people sought a distinctively Taiwanese identity. Also notable was the democratization of Taiwan, which had been under the dictatorial rule of the Kuomintang (KMT) party since the end of the 1940s, when Chiang Kai-shek moved to Taiwan. The combination of democratization and the new nationalism among the Taiwanese profoundly alarmed China, which feared that Taiwan might eventually declare its independence. China had made it clear on numerous occasions that if Taiwan were to declare independence, invite intervention by foreign powers, or indefinitely refuse to seek a resolution of the reintegration issue, then China would be compelled to resort to the use of force against Taiwan. Perhaps in order to give credence to its position and to impress its seriousness on the Taiwanese, who were holding their first presidential election, China carried out a military exercise that involved launching missiles into the vicinity of Taiwan in the spring of 1996. Thus the Taiwan Strait, which had remained in relative tranquility since the 1950s, reemerged as the most volatile flashpoint in Asia Pacific.

Perceptions of Threat and Policy Debate in Japan

In the early 1990s, whenever China was discussed in international seminars and conferences, two diametrically opposed arguments usually were presented regarding the future threat that China might pose. The first argument was that eventually China was likely to face uncontrollable domestic turmoil, triggered, perhaps, by rising demand inside China for democratization, or by serious tension arising out of the ever-widening disparity between the prosperous coastal areas and the backward inland areas, or simply by a mix of various sources of popular discontent, which could become dangerously amplified in the process of dynamic change. This argument stressed that such a scenario was bound to have a huge destabilizing impact on the security of all Asia. The other argument assumed that China would continue its robust economic development and that China's eventual emergence as the manufacturing center of the global economy would force drastic structural changes in international trade and finance, forcing painful adjustments in the economies of advanced industrial nations. It also was argued that such economic development would enable China to devote substantial resources to improving its military capability, which could become a destabilizing factor in Asia Pacific.

The second argument now appears to predominate, perhaps because of the continued dynamism of the Chinese economy throughout the 1990s. In any event, the real question is whether one considers China's failure or its success to be the threat. The common denominator seems to be China's sheer size—not so much the vastness of its territory as its huge population. And it is clear that whether one is inclined to buy one argument or another, the way China pursues modernization is destined to have huge impact not only on East Asia but on the whole world.

The following four issues have been hotly debated in Japan in the context of the perception of threat roughly described above. They relate closely to various key parameters of Japanese foreign policy discussed in chapter 1.

ODA for China

In contrast to the support among the Japanese people in the early 1980s for ODA for China, today vociferous criticism often is expressed. In essence, it asserts that Japan should stop giving large amounts of ODA to China for three reasons: First, giving China economic assistance is tantamount to subsidizing the massive buildup of its military sector, which increasingly is becoming a threat to Japan's security. Second, China gives assistance to many other developing countries, and there is no need to assist any country that can afford to assist others. Third, China does not appreciate Japan's assistance.

The counterargument maintains that China, in its deepening economic interdependence with the rest of the world, can be expected to play by the rules of the international system. Helping China in its effort to promote economic development is in the interests of Japan because the emergence of a prosperous and stable China would have a favorable impact on regional stability and prosperity, and because Japan's assistance would cement the friendly relations between the two countries and atone somewhat for the damage done in the first part of the twentieth century.

The first argument can be considered a combination of the anti-engagement school of policymaking and resentful nationalism, while the second sets forth the classical engagement policy, with the major emphasis on the role of Japan's assistance.

The Economic Rationale

What sort of economic relations with China are likely to be in the best economic interests of Japan has been debated for some time, against the backdrop of the vast expansion in trade and investment between the two countries in the 1990s. Skeptics have argued that the continued shifting of manufacturing facilities to China will accelerate the hollowing out of the manufacturing sector in Japan and seriously undermine the strength of the Japanese economy. Moreover, they see no reason to get too excited about the prospects of the Chinese economy. Proponents of engagement have argued that there is nothing wrong with shifting manufacturing to China; they point out that it is a logical outcome of a functioning market economy, in which China's lower labor costs are the decisive factor. In view of the vast potential of the Chinese market, they find it natural for Japanese businesses to deepen their economic engagement with China through direct investment and trade. Since the end of the 1990s, the second argument has gained predominance in Japan, and in the past couple of years a new wave of Japanese investment in China has begun to pick up momentum.

In 2001 Japan invoked safeguards against a number of agricultural imports, such as mushrooms and onions, from China, where production of these items had been initiated by Japanese companies that found costs to be much lower than in Japan. In response, China pointed out that being able to purchase a better product at a lower price was certainly in the interests of the Japanese consumer. China's rebuttal sounded strangely familiar to the Japanese, who had made the same argument again and again to the Americans in the 1970s and the 1980s, when friction over trade issues was high. For the farmers who were hard hit by the sharp increase in competitive imports from China, it was a life-or-death matter. The Japanese companies that had initiated production in China were treated as if they were traitors by some members of the parliament, who were committed to the defense of Japanese agriculture.

Although trade issues can easily be played up by the media or by politicians as a zero-sum game—as witnessed during the long-running trade disputes between Japan and the United States—one should not lose sight of the fact that trade is basically a plus-sum game. A country cannot improve its position by terminating its economic relations with other countries.

The History Issue

In the clash between apologists and nonapologists, discussed in chapter 1, the nonapologists' argument regarding Japan's past aggression toward China has been that enough is enough; although China may persist in playing the history card, Japan is not obliged to give any more apologies. The apologists' rebuttal has been that Japan must not forget the atrocities it committed in China in the prewar era and that it must be mindful of the sensitivity of the Chinese to this issue. The debate as to the propriety of official visits by Prime Minister Junichiro Koizumi to Yasukuni Shrine is a case in point. This memorial to Japan's war dead includes some individuals who were convicted of war crimes, and the Chinese government has strongly protested the visits.

Taiwan

Since the normalization of relations between Japan and China in 1972, an influential group of parliamentarians has remained staunchly supportive of Taiwan. Democratization in Taiwan and the new trend toward pursuit of a distinctly Taiwanese identity have strengthened their pro-Taiwan stance. The gist of their argument is that by unduly restricting relations with Taiwan and prohibiting any official contact, such as mutual visits of high-ranking government officials, the Japanese government has been too subservient to Beijing. Japan should boldly upgrade its relations with

Taiwan, which has become an outstanding example of a democratic country and one whose legitimacy increasingly is accepted in the international community. The counterargument is that Japan should observe its understanding with China that its relations with Taiwan are to be strictly nongovernmental and that it should in no way espouse the so-called two-China formula. It is not in the interest of Japan to disrupt its friendly relations with China by deviating from this basic stance; moreover, supporting the two-China formula could dangerously destabilize the Taiwan Strait.

Key Parameters of Japan's China Policy

In assessing the validity of the threat perception as well as the various policy arguments sketched above, it is important to reflect on the future prospects of a number of key parameters regarding Japan's China policy.

Values, Nationalism, and Political Systems

Since the ideology of communism has lost its legitimacy as the foundation of the Communist Party, the party's monopoly on power in China can be justified only by the achievement of the economic well-being of the people. For that purpose, Deng Xiaoping boldly accepted economic freedom as the centerpiece of his reform measures, which were bound to usher in the rebirth of capitalism. It seems inevitable, however, that freedom in the economic realm, in which individual initiative is the key to success, eventually will spill over to the political realm. Compared with the situation in the 1960s and the 1970s, marked improvement has been achieved with regard to the degree of political freedom in China. Nevertheless, the Chinese system juxtaposes almost complete freedom in the economic realm against the Communist Party's monopoly on political power. In the aftermath of the Tiananmen incident, Chinese authorities expressed both their concern and disdain that Western nations were trying to impose their democratic views on China. However, the question is not whether democratization is imposed by outside powers but whether the Communist Party can continue to rely on popular support for, or at least acquiescence to, its political control by fostering economic prosperity, reducing government corruption, promoting some degree of democratization at the local level, and widening the basis of the party by accepting the participation of "capitalists."

In East Asia in the 1960s, 1970s, and much of the 1980s, dictatorial regimes were instrumental in promoting economic development. However, successful economic development eventually produced a sizable new middle class, which became the standard-bearer of democratization. Thus, toward the end of the twentieth century, the process of democratization was under way in South Korea, Thailand, and Taiwan, among others, and everyone was hoping for the success of the nascent democracy in Indonesia. Whether a similar evolution will take place in China is a question that fascinates foreign observers, and perhaps the Chinese as well. The difficulty is China's sheer size. One can hypothesize that the larger the population, the more difficult it is to achieve democratization. Chinese leaders seem to share an obsessive fear of losing control of their vast country and triggering the type of nationwide chaos that occasionally brought enormous suffering to the country in the past. Certainly the reaction of the party leaders to Falun Gong, a quasi-religious sect, can be explained by their concern about a possible repetition of the religious upheavals, such as the Boxer Rebellion of 1900, that China has experienced in the modern era. Furthermore, the possibility of China's disintegration must have haunted its leaders as they witnessed the disintegration of the Soviet empire into fifteen sovereign states.

The question of whether China will come to share the basic values of democratic countries in North America, Europe, and Asia, including Japan, is an extremely important one. (These values used to be called Western. But today, so many countries in various parts of the world share the same basic democratic values that the validity of the description is doubtful.) This question relates closely to the perception of China as a threat to international peace and security. Certainly the seemingly irreversible trend of recent years is that through the deepening and widening of the economic interdependence among nations, China has come to have huge shared interests with democratic countries. China's accession to the WTO was the defining event in this regard. The shared interests encompass not only the economic realm but perhaps the security realm as well, inasmuch as China needs a peaceful international environment in which to pursue its quest for modernization. Nevertheless, China has yet to reach the stage in its relations with democratic nations that it shares not only interests but also basic democratic values. That may be part of the reason why the perception of China as a threat has a certain degree of resonance among democratic nations, inasmuch as it is axiomatic among them that democracies do not fight each other. It also should be noted that with ideology no longer serving as China's unifying principle, nationalism seems to be the only force that can take its place. The elation of the Chinese people over the International Olympic Committee's decision to name Beijing the host of the 2008 Olympics was one manifestation of their nationalism; the outrage over the accidental U.S. bombing of the Chinese embassy in Belgrade in 1998 was another, perhaps less benign.

It often is pointed out that to rely on nationalism in statecraft is like riding a tiger. The new leaders of China, who were installed at the sixteenth party congress, seem to be fully aware of that danger, and it seems safe to assume that their policy orientation is based on the elitism of the successful coastal area rather than on populism or nationalism. Nonetheless, managing the rising tide of nationalism continues to be a daunting task.

In sum, the interplay in China of economic freedom, the quest for democratization, the determined efforts of the government to maintain the dominance of the Communist Party, and rising nationalism is likely to determine the evolution of the political process in China over the next couple of decades.

China's Posture toward the Rest of the World

As one interpretation of the Chinese name for China, "Middle Kingdom," suggests, China has seen itself as the center of the universe for thousands of years. All the countries and people on the periphery of China were looked upon by the Chinese as inferior, and the Chinese ruling dynasty was the source of legitimacy for leaders of surrounding vassal states. Over most of human history, Chinese civilization far surpassed that of other peoples, but with the advent of the modern age, China began to suffer immensely from the imperialistic invasions and intrusions of Europeans and the Japanese. Because for thousands of years it had been at the pinnacle of power, its ensuing humiliation was all the more profound. China had never been exposed to the type of interaction and conflict among equal sovereign states that had unfolded in Europe since the seventeenth century. In essence, China's position vis-à-vis the rest of the world was one of unchallenged supremacy or victimization by other powers. Thus far, the memory of humiliation seems to have been very important in the realm of foreign policy. One gets the impression that China's analysis of international affairs often reveals a victim mentality, although it also may be a reflection of the legacy of the great Chinese strategists, who detected all sorts of conspiracies and double-crosses in the battles among kingdoms in earlier ages. The point is that in the traditional Chinese mind-set, international affairs are addressed as zero-sum propositions and it is crucially important to avoid becoming a victim of foreign conspiracies. It therefore must be somewhat difficult for China to play an entirely new game in which international economic interdependence is the key feature—and essential to China's future prosperity. Nevertheless, as far as the economic realm is concerned, China has seemed to be willing to discard the traditional mind-set in favor of becoming an active player in the game of globalization.

The Military Equation and Taiwan

Today, depending on the prism through which one observes China's evolution, entirely different images emerge. Through the prism of economics, China's ever-deepening interdependence with the rest of the world appears to be an irreversible process, and indispensable if it hopes to achieve prosperity. However, through the prism of military affairs, a different image emerges. According to a report prepared by the U.S. Department of Defense in July 2002, China's defense expenditures were more than twice as large as officially disclosed; the report also indicates that China is eager to attain the military capability required to adopt a coercive approach in its dealings with other countries.[1] Many China-watchers share the impression that China, obsessed with the possibility of humiliation, believes it imperative to vigorously pursue the modernization of its military. China seems to believe that its military strength should be proportionate to its national power—that, simply put, the military should grow in tandem with the national economy.

In the game of imperialism, military strength undoubtedly was essential in securing opportunities for economic expansion. However, in the new game of economic globalization, the role of the military is rather limited. Any country should, of course, be well prepared to deal with possible threats from what are termed rogue countries or from terrorists. But a classical military confrontation between major powers to secure their economic interests looks unlikely, simply because resorting to warfare for that purpose would be totally counterproductive and unnecessary in the global economy. It seems a bit paradoxical, then, that a nation would

---

1. U.S. Department of Defense, *Annual Report on the Military Power of the People's Republic of China* (July 2002) (www.defenselink.mil/news/Jul2002/d20020712china.pdf [June 24, 2003]).

invest a considerable portion of its economic resources in the military sector when economic development can be achieved through active participation in the process of globalization, which is characterized by interdependence and shared interests. In the case of China, the government seems to wish to prepare for contingencies involving the issue of sovereignty, which any country would be prepared to deal with seriously, including, if necessary, by the use of force. China, however, seems unique in its fear of national disintegration. Throughout the 1990s, disintegrating seemed to be the vogue in a number of countries, among them the Soviet Union and Yugoslavia. It must have been horrifying for Chinese leaders to witness this process; furthermore, it must be worrisome that today the trend seems to be to accord international legitimacy to secessionist groups and ethnic independence-seekers as long as they represent the will of the majority of the population in the region in question. Taiwan is a case in point. As mentioned, China has made it clear that if Taiwan opts for independence, invites foreign intervention, or indefinitely defers resolution of the issue, China would be compelled to resort to force. For quite some time, the tacit assumption had been that since an invasion by the People's Liberation Army (PLA) to seize Taiwan was doomed to be unsuccessful, the stalemate was likely to persist. However, as the DOD report points out, China's ongoing buildup of short-range missiles, apparently to inflict huge casualties on Taiwan, might alter this state of affairs. Furthermore, Taiwan's increasing direct investment in China means that Taiwan may become easy prey to Chinese economic intimidation.

In the past, the United States adhered to a policy of strategic ambiguity, not disclosing what it intended to do in the event of a military operation by PLA against Taiwan. The idea was to neither encourage Taiwan to opt for independence nor give China any incentive to take military action. However, presumably in response to China's buildup of missiles and in order to minimize the risk of China's miscalculating U.S. intentions, the United States now is expressing a somewhat stronger stance on the defense of Taiwan.

Japan has a vital stake in the maintenance of peace in the Taiwan Strait. Any outbreak of hostilities between U.S. forces and PLA would be truly nightmarish for Japan; moreover, it would shatter the existing international environment, which has been so favorable for the economic development of the countries in the region, including China. It is extremely important, therefore, that both parties agree to settle the issue by peaceful means. The democratization of Taiwan, though in itself a laudable development, has further complicated resolution of the issue. The Taiwanese are more likely than were the residents of Hong Kong to adamantly refuse to accept the rule of the Chinese Communist Party. Still, in order to avoid catastrophe, a patient yet imaginative approach by both sides is desperately needed.

Some Conclusions

It is amazing to observe that while the economic interdependence of Japan and China deepens and widens, the sense of nationalism in each country often manifests itself in the form of negative attitudes toward the other. This is extremely unfortunate, for both. Furthermore, the prospect of hostilities in the Taiwan Strait in which U.S. forces stationed in Japan engage in military action against China continues to haunt the Japanese. It is of paramount importance, therefore, for both Japan and China to approach their various mutual challenges and problems with the firm conviction that they have a huge shared interest in working together—and to resolve that their relationship will never be allowed to drift toward enmity because of their failure to manage their own nationalism.

6 Japan's Southeast Asia Policy

J apan has invested considerable political capital in Southeast Asia. Even back in the 1950s, Japan made a conscious effort to strengthen its economic ties with the region in the hope of compensating for the loss of the Chinese market, which absorbed a substantial portion of Japanese exports before World War II. A total of $1.5 billion in war reparations paid from 1955 to 1977 to several countries in the region—Indonesia, the Philippines, Burma, and South Vietnam—facilitated the resumption of Japanese trade. Since the 1960s, Japan has taken a series of initiatives to launch regional economic cooperation schemes. For example, Japan played the leading role in establishing the Asian Development Bank (ADB), which began operations in 1966. Japan also took the initiative in convening the Ministerial Conference for Agricultural Development in Southeast Asia in the same year. As a result of that conference, a special fund for agricultural development was established in the ADB. It was during this period that Japan began to provide government loans on concessionary terms to the countries in the region, and following establishment of the Asian Development Bank in 1966, Japan and the

United States became the leading subscribers of capital. Japan's decision to give high priority to Southeast Asia—by supporting various regional endeavors, in particular the Association of Southeast Asian Nations (ASEAN), as well as by initiating economic assistance programs for the countries in the region—was based on several considerations.

First, as the Vietnam War intensified, the sound economic development of the rest of Southeast Asia was considered essential to avoid any domino effect of the events in Indochina; it also was hoped that by enhancing the sense of solidarity among Southeast Asian countries, they would have a better chance of fending off any such effect. Second, because Japan's Official Development Assistance (ODA) program was still in its infancy, instead of spreading a comparatively small amount of assistance around the world, it seemed more effective to concentrate on a limited number of countries in Southeast Asia, where, partly because of the substantial presence of overseas Chinese merchants, the socioeconomic ethos seemed relatively well suited for economic development. Third, relations with China had yet to be normalized, and China was absorbed in the fever of the Cultural Revolution. Although normalization of relations with the Republic of Korea was completed in 1965, a number of difficulties between the two countries still had to be overcome. Under such circumstances, Japan found it much less complicated and more congenial to maintain relations with the countries of Southeast Asia.

Fourth, after the bloody upheaval in Indonesia following the expulsion of Sukarno, the situation still looked precarious, and Japan considered the need for strong support of President Suharto's new nation-building effort to be urgent. From a strategic standpoint, the stability of Indonesia has always been the key to the stability of the region as a whole. Furthermore, because the sea lane from the Indian Ocean to the Pacific goes through Indonesian waters, instability and internal strife in Indonesia could easily disrupt the flow of crude oil from the Near East to Japan. In light of that, Japan has continued to attach top priority to Indonesia in the allocation of ODA since the 1960s.

As suggested in chapter 1, ODA can easily be justified by both idealists and realists. The former can argue in this case that it is Japan's moral duty to alleviate the poverty of Southeast Asians by assisting them in their nation-building efforts; the latter can argue that it is in Japan's economic, political, and strategic interests to do so. The question is which argument is more palatable and garners more popular support. During the cold war, pacifists harbored strong negative feelings toward the very notion of strategy, which seemed to them to reflect the typical cold war confrontational mind-set. Any open admission by the government that ODA would indeed be instrumental in preventing a possible domino reaction would have triggered a tremendous domestic uproar. In order to keep things simple, the moral and humanitarian aspects of the argument justifying ODA were stressed.

The fall of Saigon and the communist takeover of Vietnam, Cambodia, and Laos heightened the sense of crisis among ASEAN countries. Since U.S. military intervention to support them in their attempts to avoid any domino effect now looked unlikely, they considered it necessary to redouble their efforts to maintain and promote their economic development and political solidarity. The catchword at the time was the "resilience" of ASEAN, meaning that through robust economic development and flexibility in managing their relations with their neighbors in Indochina, its members somehow would muddle through the crisis and not fall prey to the communists. In hindsight, the possibility that Vietnam, Cambodia, or Laos might launch an outright military intervention in Thailand, which was described as the frontline state, was extremely remote. Even so, because each ASEAN country had some significant problems—among them, indigenous insurgents—they feared that the communist regimes in Indochina might be tempted to take advantage of them in the event of internal upheaval.

In 1978, through the Fukuda Doctrine, Japan reaffirmed its commitment to giving full support to ASEAN and urged the pursuit of peaceful coexistence between ASEAN nations and Indochina. In the same year, however, the Vietnamese invasion of Cambodia to topple the Khmer Rouge, a long-time protégé of China, derailed that pursuit for the foreseeable future. On the other hand, the nightmarish vision of a Vietnamese invasion of ASEAN countries was decisively dispelled after China's military campaign against Vietnam in 1979, which China described as "teaching a lesson" to Vietnam. As a result, a new strategic equation emerged in Southeast Asia in which China inadvertently began to assume the role of guardian of the ASEAN nations. To counter China's threat, Vietnam allowed the Soviet military to have access to facilities in Cam Ran Bay. At the time, the potential for armed conflict seemed significant. One hypothetical question in looking back at the history of the Vietnam War is whether, if one could have foreseen the eventual rupture between China and Vietnam—which, in hindsight, was not surprising in view of the thousands of years of enmity between the two countries—there was sufficient reason for the U.S. intervention in Vietnam. Of course, the conviction that led to the Vietnam War was that unless the monolith of Asian communism was checked in South Vietnam, it would eventually swallow all of Southeast Asia. If one could have been certain that the monolith was a mirage, perhaps some other approach might have been attempted. Such are the reflections, typical of hindsight, that occasionally haunt us.

Vietnam and Cambodia

A somewhat more difficult challenge for Japan than pursuing economic development through ASEAN was handling its relations with Vietnam and Cambodia. Japan joined with ASEAN in denouncing Vietnam's invasion of Cambodia in the United Nations. However, the Vietnamese action had a certain degree of legitimacy, as it halted the horrifying massacre of the Cambodian people by the Khmer Rouge and restored to normalcy much of the country, except for a region near the Thai border that remained under Khmer Rouge control. The dilemma was that while Vietnam's invasion and installation of its puppet regime could not, as a matter of principle, be condoned, forcing Vietnam to withdraw was not an acceptable solution, since it would pave the way for the immediate return of the Khmer Rouge and the likely resumption of atrocities. It also was feared that suspending economic assistance to Vietnam would lead to its increased reliance on the Soviet Union and further disrupt regional security. So, in theory, one option for Japan toward the end of the 1970s and into the early 1980s was to recognize Vietnam's puppet regime, first installed under Heng Samrin and later led by Hun Sen, and to extend ODA to Vietnam. However, since the Cambodian issue had become a point of solidarity in ASEAN and therefore a litmus test of Japan's allegiance to ASEAN, Japan refrained from pursuing that option. The issue, after all, had to be addressed basically in the context of the zero-sum game of the cold war.

The stalemate in Cambodia continued throughout the 1980s. Meanwhile, the appreciation of the yen after the Plaza Accord was signed in 1985 precipitated Japanese investment in the manufacturing sectors of ASEAN countries. Following the dynamic economic growth during the 1970s of the so-called four dragons of Asia—the Republic of Korea, Taiwan, Hong Kong, and Singapore—a second group of Asian countries, Thailand, Malaysia, and Indonesia, started to show robust growth. During the 1980s, the average annual economic growth rate of the key

Figure 6-1. *Average Annual Growth Rate of Key East Asian Countries and Areas, 1980s*

Percent

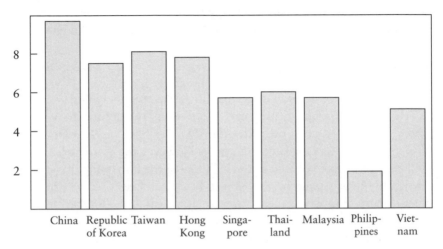

Source: *Asian Economy 2000*, Research Bureau, Economic Planning Agency of the government of Japan (June 2000).

countries of East Asia, except the Philippines, was among the highest in the world (figure 6-1). As a report by the World Bank published in 1993 pointed out, the success of all of these countries could be attributed to the economic strategy of hooking their national economies to the existing international economic system, from which they benefited enormously in terms of expanded trade and foreign investment.[1] Their success amply testified to the ineffectiveness of the alternative economic strategy of import substitution in a closed national economy, which had been tried by many developing countries in other regions.

Toward the end of the 1980s, the key players seemed to be ready to take a somewhat different approach to addressing the problem in Cambodia and the prospects of a political settlement were improving. International efforts to achieve an enduring peace in Cambodia accelerated with the end of the cold war. Japan considered working proactively for peace, which would take care of the last remnants of the war in

1. World Bank, *The East Asian Miracle* (Oxford University Press, 1993).

Indochina and effect a marked improvement in the overall security environment in East Asia, to be in its own interest. If peace was fully restored, it would become possible to invite the Indochinese countries, in particular Vietnam, to join belatedly in the dynamic economic growth being achieved in ASEAN nations. Nevertheless, relations between Japan and Vietnam were thorny toward the end of the 1980s. Japan refused to give assistance to Vietnam as long as Vietnamese troops remained in Cambodia; Vietnam responded by pointing out that it was not a beggar so eager for money that it would accept Japan's attempt to dictate its policies.

There was a tacit understanding in Tokyo that Japan would contribute a substantial amount of economic assistance to nation-building efforts in Cambodia in the event that peace was achieved, but Japan was not to be a bystander in the peace process, an uninvolved benefactor to whom the bill could be sent after the process was completed by others. At the time, there was an insistence in Japan that Japan not be taken for granted as a quiet, generous contributor to various international endeavors. Remarks such as "No taxation without representation" and "Japan is not an ATM machine" were often heard. Some foreign observers viewed Japan's proactive engagement in Cambodia as a manifestation of a new nationalism in Japan. In hindsight, certainly an element of nationalism can be seen, but it was quite different from the frustrated nationalism described in chapter 1.

Participation in the Cambodian peace process was unique among Japan's postwar foreign policy actions in terms of the country's proactive engagement in the multilateral power game, which involved a formidable assortment of players:

—*China*. The Khmer Rouge had become an increasing political liability for China. It has been speculated that since China had to improve its own image in the international community in the aftermath of the Tiananmen Square killings, it could not afford to be seen as a staunch supporter of the Khmer Rouge.

—*Soviet Union*. The Soviet Union, which would soon disappear in the early 1990s, began its military disengagement from Vietnam and the rest of Indochina. Following the communist victories in Vietnam, Cambodia, and Laos in 1975, the entire Indochina region had been seen as a huge strategic asset for the Soviets.

—*United States*. Political aversion toward Vietnam remained very strong. Sensitive issues—for example, the status of military personnel who were missing in action (MIAs)— continued to hinder the normalization of relations with Vietnam. Moreover, the United States considered Cambodia's Hun Sen unacceptable, and Vietnam was his protector. On the other hand, any notion of even remotely assisting the Khmer Rouge was rejected outright.

—*Vietnam.* Vietnam was attempting to end its international isolation by withdrawing its forces from Cambodia, perhaps having calculated that Hun Sen could survive in Cambodia without Vietnam's military backing.

—*Thailand.* Throughout the war in Indochina, Thailand feared that the war would spill over into its territory. Concluding that the possibility no longer existed, the Thai government decided to work for peace in Cambodia on the basis of its readiness to reach an eventual accommodation with Hun Sen and Vietnam. The Thai government was interested in possibilities for expanding trade with Vietnam and Cambodia, and the catchphrase of the day was "From the battlefield to the marketplace!" Moreover, it was assumed that weapons and other supplies sent to the Khmer Rouge from China were transported to the Thai-Cambodian border with the tacit acquiescence of the Thai military, which was suspected in some cases of being even more helpful. Because of this connection, the Thai military had some influence on the Khmer Rouge, whose area of control was along the Thai border.

—*France and Indonesia.* These countries acted as co-chairs of the Paris Peace Conference in 1989. As a former colonial power, France had historical ties to the region, while Indonesia acted as the de facto leader of ASEAN.

The key players in Cambodia itself before the peace process were the following:

—*Hun Sen.* He controlled most of Cambodia except the area near the Thai border held by the Khmer Rouge, and he had a strong desire to retain power. He deeply distrusted all outside powers except Vietnam, including China, the United States, and Thailand, but he was beginning to feel that Japan might be an honest broker.

—*Prince Sihanouk.* Conscious of his position as the "father of all the people of Cambodia," he was primarily concerned with establishing an independent Cambodia with himself as head of state. He deeply distrusted Hun Sen as well as the Khmer Rouge, which had killed many of his sons and other relatives.

—*Prince Ranariddh.* A son of Prince Sihanouk, he was confident that both Europe and the United States supported his faction, which was the most democratic of the four.

—*Khmer Rouge*. It realized that it was becoming more and more iso-lated, but it remained the only force that could take on Hun Sen's mili-tary. Khmer Rouge forces were regarded as superior to Hun Sen's, par-ticularly because of their guerilla tactics.

Outline of the Peace Process

The Cambodian peace negotiations resembled an effort to find a solution to an extremely complex multiple equation. Solving the multiple equation involving the international players was the easier endeavor, because all of them felt that it was high time to resolve the issue. To find a solution that would be accepted by all the players in Cambodia, however, was a truly painstaking process. Issues such as the conditions of cease-fire and the mode of disarming combatants on the battlefield were life-and-death mat-ters. There were numerous setbacks, walkouts, and boycotts, and at one point the whole process broke down temporarily. Japan developed close contact with Hun Sen in the early phases of the negotiations and urged him to accept a political compromise; Japan also had a long-standing relationship of respect and cooperation with Prince Sihanouk. These close relationships facilitated Japan's efforts to find a solution acceptable to the Cambodians, and economic assistance for nation building was another type of leverage that Japan was able to use to good effect. Although the nation-building agenda was less urgent to the Cambodians than issues such as the terms of cease-fire, it was recognized from the out-set that the international community's commitment to rebuilding Cambodia once peace was restored was an essential part of the peace process. At the Paris Peace Conference for Cambodia, Japan chaired the committee for international economic assistance and decided to con-tribute roughly half of the total requirement for the initial phase of recon-struction.

The peace agreement eventually accepted by the Cambodians stipu-lated that the UN would take responsibility for the governance of Cambodia during the transitional phase and later oversee elections to install a permanent government. Following passage of the PKO law in 1992, Japan sent its first peacekeeping personnel to Cambodia. During preparations for the elections, which were scheduled for May 1993, the Khmer Rouge dropped out of the process, and fear mounted that it might launch a full-scale military offensive to disrupt the elections. During this phase, two Japanese—an international volunteer and a civilian police officer—were killed by guerilla forces. The two deaths, which led to profound mourning among the Japanese, were described in Japan as the first Japanese war fatalities since the end of World War II. Although it was argued in the Diet that Japan should immediately withdraw its peace-keeping personnel, the government maintained its operations.

The successful resolution of the Cambodian problem made a number of positive developments in Southeast Asia possible. First, Vietnam began to attach national priority to economic development. During the first official visit of the Japanese prime minister to Vietnam in 1994, the Vietnamese noted that although Vietnam had many experts on fighting wars, it did not have many experts on nation building, and it hoped to learn from the Japanese, who had achieved extraordinary economic growth after the terrible devastation of war. Japan started to extend ODA to Vietnam in the amount of roughly a half-billion dollars a year. In the 1990s, Vietnam's economic development efforts were very similar to those of its neighbor, China. It actively engaged in foreign trade, invited foreign direct investment, and accepted the market system as the primary vehicle of modernization while the Communist Party maintained its monopoly on political power. Although the gap in per capita GDP between Vietnam and Singapore, the most advanced ASEAN country, was enormous, Vietnam joined ASEAN in 1996, followed eventually by Cambodia and Laos. By that time, perhaps most people had lost sight of the fact that ASEAN was founded to avoid the possibility that communist Vietnam might come to dominate the rest of Southeast Asia. In that sense, ASEAN's mission was fully realized with the accession of these Indochinese nations.

Foreign Policy Issues in Southeast Asia after the Mid-1990s

After the mid-1990s, Japan had to grapple with three major issues regarding Southeast Asia: political crises in Indonesia and Myanmar and the East Asian economic crisis of 1997.

Indonesia

First was the fate of Indonesia. In spite of the war in Indochina and other political upheavals, such as that during the final years of the Marcos dictatorship in the Philippines, the bottom line for the stability and security of Southeast Asia has been the stability of Indonesia, simply because of its vast size. Suharto managed to achieve considerable economic development after he became president in the 1960s. However, as his reign continued and the typical symptoms of crony capitalism started to disrupt Indonesian statecraft, whether the presidential succession could be achieved in a peaceful and orderly manner became a crucial concern. In hindsight, one is tempted to wonder whether Suharto would have stayed in power longer if the economic crisis that befell East Asia after 1997 had not occurred. In the event, the political developments that unfolded in Indonesia during that period amply testified to the validity, in its crudest sense, of the well-worn cliché that economic well-being is the prerequisite of political stability. The massive economic dislocation triggered by the East Asian economic crisis led to bloody uprisings characterized by the familiar pattern of deadly assaults on ethnic Chinese. At the height of the upheaval, Suharto was finally ousted.

Throughout this period, the most worrisome possibility was that Indonesia might disintegrate. The 1990s may in fact come to be remembered as a decade when quite a few countries proceeded to disintegrate, in part because of the end of the cold war but also because of the global trend toward intensified nationalism, which often took the form of separatist fervor. Indonesia exhibited the combination of factors most likely to exacerbate separatist sentiment, namely ethnic diversity, religious pluralism, and regional differences in the endowment of natural resources, in particular oil.

Separatist movements became quite active in various regions that had harbored resentment toward Jakarta for siphoning off the revenue that accrued from the export of local resources. Since independence, the authoritarian regime in Indonesia had managed to suppress any possible separatist movement by effective use of the military. However, as the trend toward democratization became irreversible and the Western media carried live coverage of whatever atrocity was committed, whenever and wherever, the use of brute force to suppress separatist movements became an untenable option for the government. It became increasingly evident that the Indonesian military, which had been the key to maintaining internal order and territorial integrity, could no longer function as the binding and centripetal player in the Indonesian polity. The fading away of Indonesia's authoritarian political culture, the trend toward democratization, and the diminished likelihood of brutal suppression of local upheavals were welcome developments. However, it was evident that the secession of various regions, which would in all likelihood trigger the disintegration of the nation as well as uncontrollable bloodshed, could have a devastating impact on the overall stability of Southeast Asia. Under such circumstances there was not much that foreign nations could do to help restore internal stability.

Japan had nurtured a long-standing relationship of friendship and trust with key Indonesian leaders because of the crucial role that Japan had played in Indonesia's economic development. Because of that, Japan was able to maintain close and effective contact with practically all the key players during these periods and convey its views about the ongoing crisis. What Japan did, first and foremost, was to continue to provide assistance, as further deterioration of the Indonesian economy would in all likelihood have exacerbated the political conflicts.

In the summer of 1999 Japan encountered a difficult issue that called for reconsideration of its decision to provide ODA to Indonesia. Although the Indonesian government had declared its intention to accept the independence of East Timor, it appeared that Indonesian military forces had committed atrocities in East Timor before they left the region, killing local people and burning buildings. Led by Europe, international calls for sanctions on Indonesia began to be heard in the UN and other international arenas. Obviously, such an extreme abuse of human rights could not be condoned. On the other hand, it was evident that if economic assistance to Indonesia was suspended, the swift deterioration of the Indonesian economy would inevitably follow, very likely followed in turn by nationwide bloodshed and human rights abuses on an unprecedented scale. Japan therefore worked with the United States to dissuade other countries from pushing for international economic sanctions on Indonesia.

This episode might look like a typical clash between the idealists, who believed that the international community must not condone human rights abuses, and the realists, who believed that even basic human rights should not interfere with strategic decisions. Indisputably, the imposition of economic sanctions would not have served the strategic interests of the region as a whole. However, it could be argued that continuing to extend economic assistance was necessary to avoid further bloodshed and abuse, and so could be justified from the standpoint of human rights. That, of course, does not mean that perpetrators of atrocities should be given a free hand. In the event, the serious threat of economic sanctions seemed to restrain the Indonesian military from committing further abuses.

It is encouraging to note that thus far Indonesia has managed to muddle through incessant political crises and seems to be advancing toward greater democratization. One may hope that the ethnic and religious conflicts and regional resentments in Indonesia are not as hate ridden and lethal as those witnessed in other parts of the world, such as the Balkans. If that is the case, it should be possible through the democratic process to find a compromise that can ensure the solidarity of the people and the integrity of the nation.

Myanmar

The second issue confronting Japan involved Myanmar. In 1990, the military junta, the SLORC (State Law and Order Restoration Council), held nationwide elections. When the opposition party, the NLD (National League for Democracy), led by Aung San Suu Kyi, won the overwhelming majority, the SLORC refused to accept the results. Since then, it has continued to rule by decree. It seems to be established practice in the international community not to decry or challenge a dictatorial regime unless it commits some notable human rights abuse. However, the total cancellation of the results of a lawfully carried out election was a different matter. All the major democratic countries imposed economic sanctions on Myanmar. Japan decided to suspend new ODA to Myanmar, which led to heated policy debates between the realists and idealists in the mid-1990s.

The realists reasoned that because the people of Myanmar had been extremely friendly toward Japan since the end of World War II, it did not make sense to suspend assistance and in the process throw away a friendship that was a valuable asset to Japan. Moreover, they pointed out, China had been taking advantage of Myanmar's international isolation to strengthen its influence over the country; in particular, China seemed to be trying to gain direct access to the Indian Ocean by setting up a stronghold in Myanmar, which could upset the strategic equation in the region. The United States and the European Union had no strategic interest in Myanmar, so they could afford to indulge in one-dimensional diplomacy dictated by the human rights issue, but when U.S. strategic interests were at stake, in the Korean Peninsula, for example, it was a different story: the United States supplied substantial amounts of humanitarian assistance to North Korea, in spite of the regime's record of gross abuse of human rights. To advocate the imposition of sanctions when no strategic interest was involved was a typical example of the West's double standard, which Japan should not adopt.

The idealists argued that Myanmar was an important test of Japan's commitment to basic human rights. Economic assistance for Myanmar would help no one but the ruling junta and in all likelihood antagonize the people, since it would prolong the junta's oppressive rule.

The realist argument is related to the "Asian identity versus catch up with the West" theme discussed in chapter 1. Japan continued its efforts to persuade SLORC leaders that it was in their own interest to take a more conciliatory posture, especially in easing their suppression of the opposition, so that the country could eventually escape its international isolation. Meanwhile, in 1995 Japan slightly modified its position on ODA, deciding to give some assistance on a case-by-case basis to those projects that sought to meet basic human needs, such as a nurse training program and an emergency repairs project to prevent the deterioration of airport safety. However, throughout most of the 1990s, not much progress was achieved. With the heightened tension between the SLORC and the NLD, it was truly a frustrating process.

It is always difficult to decide to what extent assistance based on humanitarian considerations should be provided to countries that abuse human rights. It can be argued that since any assistance can be interpreted as support for the abusive regime, assistance should be suspended. It also can be argued that the more oppressive the regime, the more severe the suffering of the people; in such cases, suspending humanitarian assistance results in punishing the victims, not the perpetrators, of the abuse. A recent extreme example is that of Afghanistan under Taliban rule in the late 1990s. There were widespread abuses of human rights before the Taliban was toppled by the United States and its allies in late 2001, but, commendably, international relief agencies and nongovernmental agencies (NGOs) continued to provide humanitarian assistance. The Afghan example supports the assertion that the need for humanitarian assistance is likely to be greater in countries where terrible human rights abuses are perpetrated. In countries that respect human rights, after all, the need for sustained humanitarian assistance is unusual.

The East Asian Economic Crisis of 1997

The third issue that Japan had to deal with was the aftermath of the economic crisis that suddenly engulfed all of East Asia in the summer of 1997, shattering the euphoric assumption that the region's dynamic economic growth could be taken for granted. The aggregate economic growth rate of ASEAN countries plummeted to –7.5 percent in 1998. Various factors have been identified as catalysts of this crisis, ranging from economic parameters, such as the extreme volatility of short-term capital movements, to socioeconomic shortcomings, such as crony capitalism and the lack of transparency in many countries' financial systems. As for Japan, there was no option but to do its best to prevent further deterioration of the situation. It developed a new financial assistance scheme, the Miyazawa plan, that provided $30 billion—$15 billion for meeting the mid- to long-term financial requirements of the countries in the region and another $15 billion for meeting short-term requirements—and also started to provide special "yen loans," for a total amount of as much as $5 billion, to facilitate the economic recovery of the countries in East Asia.

The recovery was faster than the pessimistic forecasts of the period indicated, thanks to, among other things, the robust North American market, which continued to absorb the exports of East Asian countries. However, it became increasingly evident that the ASEAN countries were facing a new difficulty with the emergence of China as their primary competitor in both the export market and foreign direct investment (FDI). While the difficulty that the ASEAN countries encountered during the economic crisis might have been transitory, the impact of China's economic growth on ASEAN was likely to persist. Japan, the Republic of Korea, Singapore, and Taiwan, all of which have relatively more advanced industrial sectors, have complementary trade relations with China. However, ASEAN countries such as Thailand, Malaysia, and Indonesia, whose industrial sectors are relatively less developed, are bound to have competitive trade relations with China, as their labor-intensive commodities will be exposed to severe competition from Chinese commodities in the export market. Furthermore, China emerged as the largest absorber of FDI in East Asia. In 1993, FDI in China had already overtaken aggregate FDI for the whole ASEAN region, and the gap has been growing since.

It obviously is in the interest of Japan for ASEAN to continue and to succeed in its quest for economic development in spite of the new challenges it faces. Japan has attached high priority to ASEAN in allocating ODA, and the massive flow of FDI from Japan to ASEAN countries in the late 1980s—the result of the appreciation of the yen in the aftermath of the Plaza Accord in 1985—has in effect transferred some Japanese manufacturing industries to these countries. The allocation of Japan's ODA was decided by the government, whereas the allocation of FDI was dictated by the market. Toward the end of the decade, the Japanese government began to rethink the possibility of establishing a free trade regime with its Asian neighbors. As discussed in chapter 1, since the end of World War II, avoiding isolation in the international market as other countries develop their own regional free trade agreements has been a Japanese obsession. Japan always believed that its trade interests would be best served by the global most-favored-nation system of GATT and its successor, the WTO. The traditional Japanese position has been that, pursuant to the provisions of GATT, the establishment of a free trade area would be acceptable only if the agreement covered all trade sectors, with no exceptional treatment of specific sectors, such as agriculture. It was believed that if the formation of loose free trade agreements was tolerated, they would mushroom all over the world, seriously undermining GATT, and thereby Japan's trade interests. As to Japan's options for joining a regional free trade arrangement itself, its relations with its neighbors are characterized by the vertical division of labor—unlike relations among EU countries, where horizontal division of labor is the key feature—and agriculture has always been the stumbling bloc. As the trend toward creating regional free trade associations grew during the 1990s throughout the rest of the world, Japan, China, and the Republic of Korea became the only major trading countries that were not party to any regional or bilateral free trade arrangement.

A new experimental approach was launched in the form of the Agreement between Japan and the Republic of Singapore for a New Age Economic Partnership in January 2002. In the bilateral free trade regime established under this agreement, more than 98 percent of the tariffs on trade between the two countries have been eliminated. However, the unique feature of the agreement was that it was also intended to introduce various systemic measures in both countries to promote the free flow of goods, people, capital, and information between them, strengthening their links and reducing their economic barriers. For that reason, instead of simply calling it a "free trade agreement," the countries called it an agreement for "a new age partnership." Since trade in agricultural commodities between Japan and Singapore is negligible, the agreement was much easier for the Japanese to accept. Moreover, because the two countries' per capita income is similar, horizontal division of labor is possible and various types of transborder flows can be expected to expand, to their mutual benefit. Even so, it was a marked departure from Japan's traditional policy of strict adherence to the MFN principle on a global basis.

Whether Japan should seek a much wider regional arrangement with the ASEAN countries, with the Republic of Korea and China, or with both groups depends on various factors. First, again, is the handling of the agricultural sector. Unlike Japan's arrangement with Singapore, a free trade arrangement with its other neighbors would create problems for the agricultural sector in Japan. Before deciding to accept a free trade regime with a major loophole exempting the agricultural sector, serious scrutiny is needed to determine the relative costs and benefits of deviating from the traditional rejection of such arrangements as a grave violation of the principles of GATT. There must be clear assurance that such an arrangement would not undermine the overall MFN trade system, whose survival would still be crucial to Japan. Because the ASEAN countries are at various stages of economic development, the division of labor between them and Japan would remain vertical, with the exception of Singapore. It would be far more challenging to establish a regional free trade regime or other transborder arrangement with the ASEAN countries than it was to establish the arrangement between Japan and Singapore.

7 Japan's Relations with Europe

In 1989, the Berlin Wall fell, marking the end of the cold war, and in the ensuing years Germany was united and democracy began to take hold in Russia. In Japan, however, the general perception was that although the cold war might have ended in Europe, it was far from over in Asia. It is doubtful that the cold war was a divisible commodity—that one half could have ended while the other half endured. Nevertheless, a number of developments in Asia underlay the predominance of that perception in Japan.

First, there was the Tiananmen massacre in 1989. This incident left many in Japan with no doubt that the oppressive and totalitarian nature of communism in Asia remained intact. Second, there was worrisome uncertainty over the state of affairs in the Korean Peninsula, which seemed to be a much more dangerous place in the wake of the cold war. Third, in the early 1990s it became apparent that Russia was not prepared to resolve the issue of the Northern Territory, discussed later in this chapter, as Japan had hoped. For these reasons, many Japanese felt that although Europe had a lot to be happy about, there was nothing much to celebrate in Asia.

Since the cold war began in Europe, sparked by the possibility of the communist takeover of many European countries, including Greece and Italy, and since the central issue of the cold war had always been the division of Germany, it was natural that the end of cold war should represent the resolution of European issues. Still, those essentially European issues had a huge impact on relations between Europe and Japan.

The Western European Countries

Today, as former Eastern European countries begin to participate in the dynamic process of European regional integration, the notion of Western Europe has lost much of its relevance. But during the cold war era, Western Europe constituted a distinct political entity. Japan's relations with the West Europeans can be described along three dimensions.

Politically, West Europeans were perceived in Japan as very important members of what was described as the free world—or simply as the West—of which Japan also was a member. After all, it was the West Europeans, the North Americans, and the Japanese who adhered to the values of freedom, democracy, and the open market throughout the post–World War II era. Although the West Europeans were not Japan's allies, Western Europe and Japan shared the same adversary, the Soviet Union. Any development in the realm of security in Europe was bound to affect Asian security because of the geopolitical contours of Western Europe and Japan and those of the Soviet Union, which lies between the two. A case in point was the issue of intermediate-range nuclear ballistic missiles in the first half of the 1980s. It was clear from the outset that if, in a compromise between the Soviet Union and the West, Soviet SS-20 missiles were to be withdrawn from the European theater and transferred to the far eastern part of the Soviet Union, Japan's security was bound to be affected adversely. That was part of the reason why Prime Minister Yasuhiro Nakasone took the initiative in affirming the indivisibility of the West at the Williamsburg summit in 1983. Although at the time nobody had the slightest notion that the cold war would end in the next six to seven years, in hindsight it is evident that the sense of solidarity among the political leaders of the West—Ronald Reagan, Margaret Thatcher, Helmut Kohl, and Nakasone—was instrumental in precipitating the beginning of the end of the cold war.

Economically, the picture was different. Throughout the 1980s the Western European countries became increasingly alarmed by the competitiveness of Japanese products in the global market. The trade deficit of the European Union with Japan had become persistent. The government of Japan had to devote a considerable amount of energy to diffusing trade friction with the United States, described in chapter 3, but trade talks between Japan and the EU also were often marred by a quasi-adversarial tone. Many Europeans believed that because of the U.S.-Japanese alliance, Japan was much more forthcoming in dealing with its trade issues with the United States than with Europe. They grumbled that in contrast to Europeans, who attached top priority to improving their quality of life, the Japanese devoted all the economic resources they accrued from their aggressive pursuit of exports not to enjoying their lives but to further strengthening Japan's competitive edge. For example, commenting on the often small and shabby houses in Japan, a European politician described the Japanese as living in "rabbit hutches." The joke among many Japanese exasperated by the exorbitant price of real estate was that upon hearing that comment, Japan's rabbits, whose hutches were more luxurious than Japanese houses, were thoroughly indignant.

Culturally, a strong bond existed between Europe and Japan. From the time that Japan began to modernize, much of its cultural borrowing was from Western European countries. Although after World War II there was a massive inflow of U.S. culture, many Japanese continued to have a predilection for things European, whether French art or English literature.

Whether a similar feeling existed among average Europeans toward things Japanese is debatable. Perhaps the relationship was indeed asymmetrical. Still, the Japanese were impressed with the depth of the intuitive understanding among many leading European intellectuals of various aspects of Japanese culture. It may have resulted in part from Europeans' exposure to different cultures throughout the world while they were actively pursuing their imperialist ambitions; it also may have been because they had to overcome their own cultural differences in their quest for regional integration, and so developed an appreciation of cultural diversity.

In the post–cold war era, Japan has been constantly fascinated by regional integration in Europe. That practically all the former Warsaw Pact countries are in the process of joining the European Union is a truly wonderful and logically inevitable outcome of the end of the cold war. One is deeply impressed by the determined efforts of countries trying to join the EU not only to sort out their own economic systems but also to firmly establish and enshrine basically democratic systems of government. Perhaps one of the reasons why Japan is so impressed with this process is its marked contrast to the situation in Asia, which seems unlikely to witness a similar scenario in the foreseeable future. Eventually, of course, there may be a free trade area encompassing most of East Asia, including Japan, China, the Korean Peninsula, and the ASEAN countries. Even so, the degree of integration would be different. No Asian regional endeavor is likely to have the equivalent of the EU's central governing body, located in Brussels. The crucial difference is the absence of the shared values that are the hallmark of the European endeavor.

Japan has been watching the emergence of a common foreign policy among the EU nations with a mix of fascination and skepticism. As Japan sees it, it is one thing for the members of the EU to agree on economic policies among themselves, but it is a totally different matter for these countries, which originated the practice of realpolitik, to agree on foreign policy. One may call this skepticism a hangover of the cold war. During the cold war, the United States always raised grand ideals to rally the free world, while the Europeans, who had been practicing the game of realpolitik for centuries, coolly counseled the Americans on the correct conduct of the war and all other strategic challenges. After all, whereas the United States was founded on basic values, the European countries today are the outcome of the interplay of realpolitik among sovereign states since the seventeenth century.

Japan speculated that a common foreign policy might be formulated by taking the average of the policy pronouncements of all member states, but it could not help but wonder how the art of realpolitik, a uniquely European product, could be served by calculating an average. The common denominator, however, appears to be the Europeans' shared values. Japan became aware of this evolution toward the end of the 1990s, when the G-8 nations had to find a common approach to dealing with the many instances of human rights abuse all over the world. After the NATO bombing in Kosovo in 1998, in particular, the EU seemed to start taking a tougher posture toward perpetrators of all kind of human rights abuses, by advocating, for example, the imposition of economic sanctions. In a sense, the Europeans sounded more Wilsonian than the Americans. Meanwhile, in East Asia grumbling was heard: the Europeans were eager to introduce economic sanctions in dealing with cases like East Timor and Myanmar only because they no longer had a strategic stake in East Asia.

Another defining issue was the war against Iraq in 2003. The predominant view in Europe was that without the authorization of the UN Security Council, military action by a UN member state should not be permitted. In a brilliant essay, Robert Kagan described "a powerful European interest in inhabiting a world where strength doesn't matter, where international law and international institutions predominate, where unilateral action by powerful nations is forbidden, where all nations regardless of their strength have equal rights and are equally protected by commonly agreed-upon international rules of behavior."[1] Kagan focused primarily on the Atlantic Alliance. However, how the Europeans behave in their quest for peace or in managing their relations with the United States is bound to have an extremely important bearing on Japan's foreign policy as well. Although the context is different from that of the cold war era, peace is no more a divisible commodity than war is; with globalization, the Atlantic nations cannot pick up the option on peace and leave conflict to Asia and the Pacific.

In the mid-1990s, the concept was floated of cross-regional cooperation between the EU and Japan on geopolitical issues. The idea was that Japan would play a more active role in resolving problems in the Balkans, such as the violence in Bosnia, while the EU would be actively involved in security challenges in East Asia, such as the situation in the Korean Peninsula. In Japan, the view was that the Balkans was exclusively a European problem. Even so, because the way the Balkan problems were resolved was bound to set precedents regarding the making of rules to ensure international peace and security—and because Japan and the EU shared basic values and interests—Japan decided to make a significant financial contribution to support post-conflict operations in Bosnia.

The EU, for its part, decided to join KEDO (Korean Peninsula Energy Development Organization), which was set up to implement the construction of a light-water reactor in North Korea pursuant to the Agreed Framework of 1994. Japan pointed out that if the development of nuclear weapons in North Korea remained unchecked, the threat would not be confined to East Asia—that the most likely market for nuclear weapons would be the Gulf and the Middle East, in which the EU had a huge geostrategic interest that was likely to be adversely affected. It was joked that Japan was coercing the EU on behalf of North Korea to chip in on financial contributions to KEDO.

In the economic arena, it has been absolutely essential for Japan to work with the Europeans. In the realm of international rule making in particular, such as the rounds of negotiations in the World Trade Orga-

1. Robert Kagan, "Power and Weakness," *Policy Review*, no. 113 (June–July 2002).

nization, close contact with the EU has become indispensable for Japan. Since the end of the cold war, the Europeans and the Japanese have shared the conviction that they should strengthen their working relationship. The perception in Japan, however, was that because the Europeans were so preoccupied with deepening and widening the EU, their relations with Japan and Asia as a whole could command only a moderate share of their attention. In order to address this problem, Japan and the EU adopted a plan set forth in a document entitled *Shaping Our Common Future: An Action Plan for EU-Japan Cooperation* during their summit meeting in December 2001.[2] The plan appears to cover virtually every type of challenge facing the world today. It defines four major areas of interest: peace and security; strengthening economic and trade partnerships by using globalization to the benefit of all; coping with global and societal challenges; and bringing people and cultures together. It is hoped that the plan will serve not as a mantra to be recited on special occasions but as a guideline for concrete, proactive follow-up action by both parties.

Russia

Russia has always occupied a special place in Japan's relations with the European world because of its geographical proximity. As the eastward expansion of Russia reached the Pacific coast of the Eurasian landmass, Russia became one of Japan's nearest neighbors. Even before Commodore Matthew Perry forced the Tokugawa shogunate to open Japan, there were a series of attempts by the Russians to establish contacts with Japan in the first half of the nineteenth century. After the Meiji Restoration, as Japan belatedly but actively participated in the imperialist games on the Asian continent along with the European powers, it was primarily the Russian advance toward Manchuria and the Korean Peninsula that collided with Japan's interests. Long after the Russo-Japanese War of 1904–05, Russia was considered Japan's primary potential adversary by the military planners in the Japanese Imperial Army.

In August 1945, when the defeat of Japan looked imminent, the Soviet Union, in gross violation of the two countries' treaty of neutrality, launched a military campaign against Japan and occupied the Northern Territory in what was generally perceived as a land grab a few weeks

2. *Shaping Our Common Future: An Action Plan for EU-Japan Cooperation* (http://europa.eu.int/comm/external_relations/japan/intro/summ_index.htm [June 25, 2003]).

after Japan's capitulation. The Soviets also took a huge number of Japanese soldiers as prisoners of war to Siberia, where many of them perished doing forced hard labor. This series of actions created a deep well of negative feeling among the Japanese people toward the Soviets.

As described in chapter 2, Prime Minister Shigeru Yoshida opted for forming security ties with the United States. Although the leftists criticized the San Francisco Peace Treaty as a U.S. ploy to enlist Japan in a dangerous confrontation with the Soviets, the alternatives, such as unarmed neutrality or the maintenance of equivalent relationships with the United States and the Soviets, never held any appeal for Yoshida and his successors in the conservative leadership. Still, Prime Minister Ichiro Hatoyama, who succeeded Yoshida, managed to normalize Japan's relations with the Soviet Union in 1956 by signing a joint declaration in which the state of belligerency between the two countries was formally terminated. However, they did not conclude a peace treaty because of their territorial dispute regarding the Soviets' continued occupation of the Northern Territory. In the joint declaration the Soviets pledged to return the two small islands of Habomai and Shikotan when a peace treaty was concluded. The Japanese insisted that unless and until not only those but also two other islands, Kunashiri and Etorofu, were returned, no peace treaty with the Soviet Union could be signed. In the event, after the revision of the U.S.-Japanese security treaty in 1960, the Soviets rescinded their pledge to return the two islands and claimed that no territorial issue existed between the two countries.

Throughout the cold war era, some economic interaction between the two countries continued. In particular, the Soviets allowed Japan to fish the waters off the Pacific coast of the Soviet Union, which was very important to the Japanese fishing industry. In the 1970s, some joint projects were attempted to develop natural resources, such as natural gas, oil, and timber, in Siberia. However, the two countries' relations were conducted within the overall context of the cold war, in which the prospects for a real breakthrough looked dim. Moreover, as the Soviet posture toward Japan often was high-handed and coercive, the negative feeling among the Japanese toward the Soviets persisted. In the realm of security, Japan's defense planning was based on the assumption that in the event of a global military conflict between the West and the East, the Soviet Union was likely to launch a campaign to occupy Japan's northernmost island, Hokkaido, and to try to gain control of the three Japanese straits that constitute exits for the Soviet naval force to the Pacific Ocean.

Naturally Japan was fascinated by the demise of the Soviet empire in the early 1990s. In the beginning, as various attempts were made to reintroduce the familiar games of the old regime, the extent to which democracy was going to take in Russia was uncertain. Nevertheless, the country's success in maintaining political pluralism was quite impressive, even if its introduction of a market economy was less so. At the time, China had started to accelerate its efforts toward full adoption of the market mechanism. One wondered which of the two, Russia or China, was the hare and which the tortoise in their quest for reform. In the economic race, China obviously was the hare and Russia the tortoise. In the race toward democratization, Russia appeared to be quite a dynamic hare. The final goal was a bit unclear, but it was fascinating to witness Japan's two huge neighbors conducting their grand experiments simultaneously.

In Japan there was a widespread expectation that with the collapse of the communist regime in Russia, the Northern Territory dispute would finally be resolved. However, a rising tide of nationalism had begun to fill the vacuum created by communism's demise. It became increasingly clear that the resolution of the territorial dispute, which could easily trigger a surge of angry nationalism, was becoming a difficult and sensitive issue for the Russian government. The Russians seemed prepared to return the two islands as stipulated in the Joint Declaration of 1956, as long as Japan accepted that gesture as the final resolution of the territorial issue. However, since Japan could not accept such a resolution—and continues to adhere to the position that all four islands must be returned—negotiations will have to continue.

Meanwhile, since the inception of the Russian Federation, considerable progress has been made in relations between Japan and Russia. In the economic arena, a series of both government and business initiatives have been taken to promote economic transactions between the two countries. Although Japanese exports to and direct investment in Russia started to pick up toward the end of the 1990s, in 2001 Japan ranked ninth among Russia's world trade partners, with a 2.4 percent share of overall trade. In view of the abundant undeveloped natural resources in Siberia and the high level of scientific and technological knowledge in Russia, there remains vast potential for the expansion of Russo-Japanese economic relations. Japanese business has not been as forthcoming in investing in Russia as it has in China, due perhaps to the perception in Japan that the overall structure of Russia's economic system is not yet adequate for active foreign investment.

It has become increasingly important for Japan to work with Russia in addressing various security issues, such as the international fight against terrorism, and regional tensions, such as that over North Korea's development of nuclear weapons. It was in political consultations with Russia on various regional issues that Japan first felt the impact of the end of the cold war. During the cold war, their views on Asia and the Middle East had always been diametrically opposed, the inevitable result of the zero-sum game of the cold war. Since the mid-1990s, however, it has been refreshing to find that the two countries have come to share similar views and assessments of many issues.

The 9/11 terrorist attacks seem to have prompted President Vladimir Putin to undertake a strategic revision of Russia's posture toward the United States. If Russia has come to the conclusion that its security interests will be better served by closer cooperation with the rest of the world on strategic issues, then it should be possible for both Russia and Japan to widen their shared interest in the realm of peace and security, notably in the Korean Peninsula, where Russia has been one of the key players in modern history.

It is clearly in Japan's interest for Russia to strive further to cement a democratic system of governance, to solidify the market mechanism so that Russia can become an active and truly effective participant in Asian-Pacific economic prosperity, and to become, in essence, an effective stabilizing power both around the world and in Asia Pacific. And in that evolutionary process it is hoped that Russia will see it in its national interest to resolve the territorial issue with Japan, so that the countries' relations can be fully normalized. Strobe Talbott, who was deputy secretary of state during the Clinton administration, recounted that in the early 1990s the United States tried to persuade Russia to take a particular course of action on many issues by stressing that was in the interest of Russia to do so—so often, in fact, that the Russians responded that they hated to be reminded of the Russian interest.[3] He described this process as the "spinach treatment," as when parents urge their children to eat spinach so that they will grow up to be big and strong. It is totally unclear whether a similar spinach treatment by Japan will be effective. Still, it seems that the surest way to achieve progress in international relations in the post–cold war world is to try to deepen and widen the sharing of interests and values among all nations.

3. Strobe Talbott, *The Russia Hand* (Random House, 2002).

8 | *Striving for Peace and Saving Failed States*

The preceding chapters present various options for addressing issues that directly affect the security of Japan, focusing primarily on familiar strategic subjects such as the security ties between Japan and the United States, the political situation in the Korean Peninsula, and Sino-Japanese relations. This chapter explores Japan's role in UN peace efforts, presents several scenarios of crises that could befall Japan in the future, and closes with some comments about foreign policy challenges and options in the coming years.

Japan's Role in UN Peace Efforts

It seems important to explore how Japan can play a proactive role in efforts to restore states and areas in which the whole framework of nationhood has collapsed because of internal conflicts or other catastrophic events. Although the failure of faraway states may not directly affect Japan's security, it is nonetheless in Japan's interest to support international efforts to minimize the destabilizing impact of state collapse wherever it occurs. As the case of

Afghanistan in the 1990s amply testified, failed states may become fertile ground for the growth of terrorist organizations, whose actions can have disastrous effects on world stability.

It is necessary, and in some cases essential, to use some degree of force to impose peace and restore order in cases of state collapse, whether this is done by the UN or other states. During the cold war, the role of the UN was limited to peacekeeping operations in which the use of force basically was precluded. In essence, peacekeeping forces were to be dispatched only after peace was restored, to ensure that peace agreements between former enemies were observed; they were not meant to enforce the peace. The limits of UN peacekeeping operations were made painfully clear during the tragic war in Bosnia in the early 1990s, when it became apparent that some sort of new international system had to be developed whose function was not to keep the peace but to enforce it. And if that role was to be performed by the UN, obviously the UN should be equipped with its own armed force, as envisaged in Chapter 7 of the UN Charter.

When the cold war ended, there was some expectation that, at long last, the United Nations would in fact have its own armed force. For example, in 1992, a UN report proposed forming a peace-enforcing unit that would consist of troops earmarked and made readily available for operations commanded by the Secretary General.[1] It soon became apparent, however, that formation of such a force was unlikely because, in essence, major member states were unlikely to commit their troops to the command of the UN. Instead, forming—pursuant to an authorizing resolution of the Security Council—a multinational combat force in which soldiers remained under the command of their own government became the norm in dealing with failed states and related humanitarian crises. Whether Iraq in 1990 should be defined as a failed state may be debatable. If Iraq is included in this category, however, then practically all instances of war, use of force, and humanitarian disaster in the post–cold war era can be considered outcomes, in a broad sense, of state failure. The 1990s appear to have been a time when ethnic, religious, and political animosities that had been frozen during the cold war suddenly came to life. The record of the international community in grappling with the resulting crises, such as those in Cambodia, Somalia, Afghanistan, the

---

1. *An Agenda for Peace: Preventive Diplomacy, Peace-Making, and Peace-Keeping,* Report of the Secretary General, June 17, 1992 (http://www.un.org/Docs/SG/agpeace.html [June 27, 2003]).

Balkans, Rwanda, East Timor, Haiti, and Albania, was mixed. While eventually some commendable successes were achieved, for example, in Cambodia and East Timor, appalling atrocities were committed before delayed efforts were made to restore peace and order in other cases, like Bosnia and Rwanda.

The Secretary General of the UN, Kofi Annan, recounted in the late 1990s that the proportion of civilians among the total war dead for the decade was estimated to be 75 percent. In World War I, civilians accounted for 10 percent of the total war dead, and in World War II, civilians, including Holocaust victims, accounted for 50 percent of the total war dead. This horrifying increase in the proportion of civilian deaths testifies to the nature of the crisis arising from the failure of states, and there is no guarantee that such failures will subside in the coming years.

In cases of state failure, the Security Council often adopts a resolution authorizing the formation of a multinational force to enforce peace and order in a state or area where terrible atrocities have been committed or where order has completely collapsed. Such a resolution may be adopted to follow up an agreement, such as a peace accord, among the parties concerned, including the various factions within the failed state itself (Bosnia, Kosovo, and Afghanistan are typical examples). Peace negotiations, during which a political settlement must be reached among parties that strove to kill each other in the past, can be extremely difficult, and often require the patient, diligent, and innovative involvement of major powers. If the Security Council determines that a multinational force is not needed to restore order, peacekeeping troops may suffice. In Cambodia, the UN peacekeeping operation succeeded in restoring the peace after decades of genocidal war.

In parallel with the Security Council's deliberations, an international conference often is convened under the aegis of the UN in which major donor countries pledge humanitarian assistance and postwar or postcrisis reconstruction and development assistance. This sort of fund-raising has been an essential part of peace-building efforts. The assurance that the international community will provide substantial economic assistance if peace is restored often serves as an additional incentive for the warring parties to accept a peace accord.

Because new legislation would be needed to empower the Japanese government to engage the Japanese Self-Defense Force in noncombat activities to support a UN multinational force, Japan has not participated in such activities. In view of the likelihood that in the future a UN-authorized multinational force will be the key feature of international efforts to maintain order and ensure the peace, legislative initiatives on Japan's participation in those efforts should be actively examined. Although there may be another round of clashes between pacifists and realists on the constitutionality of such legislation, much of the legal argument seems to have been sorted out in the course of parliamentary debate since the late 1990s.

On the other hand, Japan has actively participated in various UN peacekeeping operations since the "PKO law" was passed in 1992, and the vociferously decried entanglement in war that was predicted to follow its passage has never materialized. It is heartening that today a majority of the Japanese people have come to consider peacekeeping operations a very important mission of the JSDF. The first instance of Japan's active participation in a negotiated peace settlement was in Cambodia, as described in chapter 6. The reasons why hatred overwhelms parties to a conflict or why order collapses in a state are so diverse that no generalizations can adequately predict or explain them. Still, it seems worthwhile for Japan to prepare to get actively involved, as it did in Cambodia, in the process of negotiating the settlement of conflicts wherever they arise.

Japan has consciously taken a proactive role in providing all forms of humanitarian and economic assistance to peace-building efforts in failed states. In the case of Cambodia, Japan bore roughly half of the costs of postconflict assistance. Japan hosted an international conference on providing relief and support to Afghanistan in January 2002, immediately after a provisional government was established there. It was encouraging to note that in spite of the growing criticism in Japan of Official Development Assistance, there was widespread support for providing substantial assistance to Afghanistan. Even though pacifists and realists may diverge in their views regarding the use of force to maintain order, there seems to be nationwide accord on the need for humanitarian and reconstruction assistance. Moreover, Japanese nongovernmental agencies have become a huge asset in assisting the recovery and nation-building efforts of failed states.

Japan and the Security Council

Although the UN force originally envisaged in Chapter 7 of the UN Charter is unlikely to be formed in the foreseeable future, it seems certain that the Security Council, the body that legitimizes the use of force by member states, will continue to play the key role in the international community's quest for peace. Of course, it also performs other functions, such as dispatching peacekeeping troops and overseeing mediation efforts to diffuse the crises and conflicts that come under its purview. Against this background the Japanese government came to the conclusion in the mid-1990s that in order to contribute proactively to the quest for peace—and in view of the fact that Japan had become the UN's second-largest contributor, bearing 20 percent of the UN regular budget—Japan should seek a permanent seat on the Security Council in the context of the council's overall reform. Many UN members had come to share the view that, a half-century after its inception, the Security Council's composition and functioning did not reflect reality in the 1990s. Therefore in the mid-1990s, serious work began in the UN to review all aspects of reform of the Security Council, such as the number of members in an expanded council, the possible allocation of permanent and nonpermanent seats for various regional groups, and the handling of veto power for permanent members. If the issue had been simply one of Japan's eligibility for a new permanent position on the council, Japan would have had overwhelming numerical support in the UN. The difficulty, however, lay in the way permanent members from various regions, such as Latin America, Africa, Asia, and Europe, were selected. In essence, a kind of numerical law of physics worked to hinder the emergence of consensus. States that had no chance of being selected as an eligible candidate from their region, which outnumbered the eligible states, were fiercely opposed to expanding the number of permanent members because it could result in the selection of their rivals. The reform of the Security Council, therefore, has become an item of unfinished business on the agenda for the new century.

In Japan, there was some opposition to the government's decision to seek a permanent seat on the Security Council. Because the constitution prohibited the use of force except in exercising the right of individual self-defense, Japan's permanent membership on the council, which was entrusted with the power to authorize war, was considered inappropriate. In response, the Japanese government clarified its position, specifying that its quest for a permanent seat was to be undertaken within the constraints of the constitution. At the time, it was argued that perhaps Japan should play the role of a "small but shining country," and inherent in the argument was some degree of psychological resistance to playing a proactive role in the realm of international peace and security. However, it was evident then, as it is today, that even if participating in the use of force by a multinational force is not an option, Japan can play a meaningful and substantial role in the quest for international peace and that such a proactive posture is both in Japan's interest and its moral obligation.

In the mid-1990s, the author had interesting informal talks with the assistant secretary in charge of Asian affairs in the British Foreign Office, who asked what sort of strategy Japan was pursuing to maintain and strengthen its influence in the international arena. The author replied that Japan had to be somewhat careful about the use of the word "influence" because it could raise sensitivities and perhaps invite a negative reaction not only from its neighbors in Asia but also within Japan. The assistant secretary observed that even though Britain's overall national strength had been waning, the need to safeguard the national interest in the international arena was growing, and that therefore maintaining British influence was all the more crucial an aspect of British foreign policy.

The fact that both France and Britain are categorically opposed to the idea of giving up their permanent seats on the Security Council in exchange for one permanent seat for the European Union amply testifies to their fear of possible encroachment on their influence. Perhaps the Japanese Foreign Ministry should have argued its case in a more straightforward manner, noting that the maintenance of international influence is essential from the standpoint of national interest and that Japan's accession to a permanent seat on the Security Council would be extremely beneficial in that regard.

Comments

These days "regime change" has become a cliché in discussions of rogue states, particularly Iraq. Hope was expressed prior to the ousting of Saddam Hussein in 2003 that the Japanese post–World War II model of governance and reconstruction would be adopted in Iraq, recasting the country as a beacon of democracy in the Middle East. It will be truly wonderful if that is how things evolve, although one can raise many points of difference between Iraq in 2003 and Japan in 1945.

Therein lies the most difficult aspect of achieving a political settlement of grievances and building the peace in the aftermath of an internal war or the deposing of a lethal despot like Saddam Hussein. Unless some form of democracy is established, the situation will not be stabilized. However, the successful introduction of democracy requires some degree of political maturity and readiness within a society to accept the basic tenets of democracy. In the late 1980s, when Mikhail Gorbachev launched his campaign of *glasnost* and *perestroika*, the inherent difficulty of changing the mentality of the Russian people, who were accustomed to taking orders from the government, was pointed out in such one-liners as "Comrade, the new order is 'Don't wait for orders!'" One can cite the case of Japan in 1945 as a successful attempt to "impose democracy," however contradictory the term may be. However, before the advent of the fanatical militarism of the 1930s, Japan had undergone a gradual but meaningful process of democratization that had begun in the late nineteenth century, along with the nation's modernization. There were no tribal, ethnic, or regional hostilities that could easily trigger massive violence among the people. The rule of law was firmly adhered to. Those were the preconditions that made the successful "imposition" of democracy possible in Japan.

Japan's Position vis-à-vis Key Phases in the Process of Saving Failed States

—*Stopping internal strife or deposing a despot.* Use of force is essential. Japan cannot engage the JSDF in the use of force.

—*Restoring order.* This includes disarming the parties to the conflict and policing the area involved, which inevitably requires the use of force. Japan may participate in those parts of operations that do not involve the use of force.

—*Financing humanitarian relief and reconstruction efforts in the post-conflict phase.* This is important in persuading parties to a conflict to accept a cease-fire agreement and a political settlement of their grievances. Japan has done a great deal in this area in the past and is expected to continue to do so.

—*Introducing/imposing democracy.* This is the most difficult part of the peace-building process, without which peace and order would remain extremely fragile. In particular, the eventual conduct of free and fair elections is essential. However, convincing the people in postconflict countries such as Iraq and Afghanistan that free and fair elections are indeed essential to restoring order and beginning the nation-building process remains a huge challenge. Japan thus far has actively participated in international monitoring of elections in post-conflict countries. Sharing the experience of Japan in 1945 would be much more difficult, but it still may be worthwhile to try.

After the NATO campaign in Kosovo, a change in international law occurred that allows the international community to use force against a sovereign state to stop terrible abuses of human rights within its borders. It is too speculative to try to gauge how many more states are likely to be the objects of such international intervention in the coming decades, or how many more are likely to join the club of rogue and failed states, becoming a security concern for the rest of the world. Nevertheless, it is likely to be one of the most significant challenges that the international community as a whole will have to address for many years to come. Japan, therefore, should be prepared to play a proactive role in supporting the political settlement of conflicts in failed states, including cease-fire and power-sharing agreements, or, if regime change does occur, in facilitating the transition to normalcy. Last, but equally important, Japan should promote the economic development of the poorer parts of the world so that the failure of states and the emergence of rogue nations can be prevented.

Hypothetical Worst-Case Scenarios

In Japan, whenever the political stakes are high, many political leaders must be included in the decisionmaking process in order to ensure that the views of all are represented and that they all share responsibility for the final decision. That is the essence of *nemawashi*, Japan's consensus-oriented culture. Because the number of players is large, the relative transparency of the process is ensured. However, when a timely decision by the leader is absolutely essential, the government must forgo the lengthy process of consensus building. Some of the hypothetical cases described below—which one hopes will never materialize—would require agonizing decisionmaking by political leaders under extreme pressure and tight time constraints. Every effort must be made to avoid such scenarios in the first place. Nevertheless, even though it may seem like sensationalist scare-mongering, it is very important for decisionmakers to keep worst-case scenarios in mind and to be psychologically prepared to deal with them. To follow up the various options on key issues that were described in the previous chapters, several possible defining crises that might befall Japan in the next couple of decades are described below.

Korean Peninsula

In the summer of the year 20XX, following the massive, unstoppable outflow of North Korean refugees into China, worsening famine, and an attempted military coup, the collapse of the regime in North Korea looks imminent. The North Korean leadership believes that South Korea and the United States are behind the deterioration of order and threatens to mount a deadly attack with conventional weapons on Seoul in twenty-four hours unless they immediately stop intervening in the North. Both South Korea and the United States declare the accusations to be totally unfounded. North Korea, however, refuses to accept their denials and seems ready to launch its threatened military action against the South. In response, the United States prepares for a full-scale military operation to minimize damage to South Korea. At that point, North Korea notifies the United States that if it takes action, North Korea will launch its previously concealed nuclear weapons against Japan. The United States immediately warns North Korea that if it uses its nuclear weapons, it will be promptly obliterated by a U.S. nuclear strike. North Korea seems to be unperturbed by the threat. It appears determined to punish South Korea, which it believes triggered the collapse of the North, even if its actions mean the end of the regime and, in effect, the country.

Taiwan Strait

In the year 20YY, a new president of Taiwan is elected. His landslide victory follows a campaign in which he repeatedly called for Taiwan's independence. He has stressed that since the 1990s the clear trend in the international community has been to accept the legitimacy of the secession of certain regions in pursuit of independence as long as the will of the inhabitants is reflected through the democratic process. As to the possible use of force by China to stop the secession of Taiwan, he expresses his confidence that in that event the United States will honor its defense commitment to Taiwan and take all necessary military measures against China. He also emphasizes his hope that all countries, including Japan, that are committed to the fundamental values of freedom and democracy will help Taiwan in its quest for independence.

China makes it very clear that if Taiwan declares independence, China will be obliged to start a military campaign against Taiwan, using all available means, including massive missile attacks. China also warns that any U.S. military intervention to assist Taiwan would lead to grave consequences. Although the outbreak of hostilities will disrupt if not destroy the international economic climate that has been so favorable to the economic development of countries in East Asia, China's leaders will not compromise on the issue of Taiwan's independence.

The United States has told Japan that the use of U.S. bases in Japan, in particular those in Okinawa, would be absolutely essential in defending Taiwan and has expressed the hope that Japan will allow their use. In the United States, the majority of the people strongly support Taiwan's independence, and many Americans resent China for its position regarding the use of military means to suppress Taiwan.

China has conveyed to Japan, in the strongest possible terms, that if Japan allows the United States to use its bases in Japan for a military operation against China, not only would relations between Japan and China be irreparably damaged, but Japan would be deemed a de facto belligerent. China sweetens its remarks by suggesting that if Japan decides not to permit the United States to use its bases and Taiwan's independence is averted, then much more fruitful relations between Japan and China can be explored, encompassing not only their existing economic ties but also close cooperation on security issues that would decisively reduce the importance to Japan of its security ties with the United States.

Indonesia

In 20ZZ, the disintegration of Indonesia begins. Many provinces that have harbored strong resentment against Jakarta defiantly declare their independence. The Indonesian military, which thus far has managed to maintain Indonesia's territorial integrity, has lost much of its effectiveness and legitimacy. The most extreme Muslim fundamentalist group has taken over the remotest part of Indonesia, taking hostage many Japanese tourists and officials who are working for aid projects there. The group notifies the Japanese government that unless Japan immediately suspends all JSDF activities supporting U.S. operations against al Qaeda, the hostages will be executed. Relying on a rescue operation by the Indonesian military does not seem to be an option.

The U.S.-Japanese Security Arrangement

In the year 20AA, the United States has become markedly introverted. The average American believes that the United States no longer needs its allies, which have been utterly unhelpful in its fight against terrorists and rogue nations. Given the preponderance of U.S. military strength, calls to return to "Fortress America" seems to be gaining widespread domestic acceptance. In Japan, the popular media has played up the idea that Japan's prolonged economic stagnation is the result of a U.S. conspiracy. Against this background, U.S. servicemen in Okinawa are accused of committing a succession of heinous crimes, triggering nationwide outrage in Japan. A national poll indicates that a majority of the Japanese feel that they cannot tolerate the U.S. bases any longer and favor the withdrawal of American forces from Japan. The U.S. public is furious because many Japanese political leaders have treated the U.S. troops as if they were a bunch of criminals. Suddenly the possibility of terminating the U.S.-Japanese security treaty becomes fiercely debated in both countries. The mood in Japan has become so emotional that any argument pointing out the strategic advantages of the treaty tends to be jeered.

Indian Ocean

In the year 20BB, after a series of coups and countercoups, a Muslim fundamentalist leader who is suspected of having close ties with the Taliban is installed as president of Pakistan. He boasts about Pakistan's nuclear weapons, which are a source of pride for the whole Muslim world. Tension with India immediately starts to rise. Because martyrdom is exalted by Muslim fundamentalists, deterrent strategies may not have much effect on the new leader. The United States cannot resort to a preemptive strike to force regime change, because it could trigger a regional nuclear war.

The Pakistani government declares that safe passage through the Indian Ocean can no longer be guaranteed for ships that belong to states "that engage in the persecution of Muslims under the pretext of fighting terrorism." Perhaps encouraged by this pronouncement, local fundamentalists using small armed ships attempt to interdict tankers and other vessels. Because oil tankers from the Gulf region en route to Japan have to pass the coast of Pakistan, this turn of events creates a serious challenge to the security of Japan. However, because the security ties between the United States and Japan were terminated in the year 20AA, Japan can no longer rely on the U.S. Seventh Fleet for protection.

Observations

—*Korean Peninsula.* The key approaches to averting crisis in the Korean Peninsula are covered extensively in chapter 4. In essence, the ongoing efforts to prevent nuclear development by North Korea are intended to avert the nuclear blackmail described in this scenario. Even if some grand bargain is eventually worked out, there would still remain the possibility of deadly disruption in the North triggered by the collapse of the regime. One can, of course, hope for a more optimistic scenario in which the nature of the regime changes over the long run and North Korea becomes a law-abiding member of the international community. Still, unless and until such a scenario becomes an irreversible reality, the potential for such a crisis will continue to haunt us.

—*Taiwan Strait*. The problems involving the Taiwan Strait are covered in chapter 5. Unlike in the case of the Korea Peninsula, they do not involve the possible collapse of the regime or, at the outset, nuclear blackmail. Crisis could be triggered by a series of miscalculations by either Taiwan or China or by both. The extent to which an emotional upsurge of nationalism in either country would escalate into a crisis would be the decisive factor. Any outbreak of armed conflict in the Taiwan Strait is bound to destroy the favorable international economic environment that has made the dynamic economic development of both China and Taiwan possible. Moreover, military intervention by the United States and the ensuing military showdown between the United States and China would be truly catastrophic, not only for East Asia but for the whole world. It therefore is unquestionably in the interests of both China and Taiwan not to cross the line beyond which armed conflict becomes unavoidable. Japan cannot easily come up with a magic formula to dispel the tension in a crisis such as this. The likely course of action would be to stress vehemently to both sides that it is not in their interests to plunge into uncontrollable armed conflict.

One can hope that in the long run, as the economic integration of the two countries proceeds, both will share a stronger interest in maintaining the status quo. If, sometime in the distant future, democratization in China is set in motion and China and Taiwan find themselves sharing a similar politicoeconomic outlook, the risk of armed conflict may finally be mitigated.

—*Indonesia*. The type of hostage taking mentioned in this scenario can and does take place anywhere in the world where local authorities are not effective in preventing terrorist activities. In that sense, the threat of terrorism today is truly global. Simply withdrawing nationals from dangerous parts of the world can be effective in avoiding such risks. Often local authorities claim that such precautionary withdrawals are not based on real dangers but on foreigners' tendency to overreact; still, "Safety first" has become the byword where the protection of nationals is concerned.

It is difficult to make meaningful generalizations about how to deal with a crisis once hostages have been taken, since a lot depends on the details of the situation. No one can determine the feasibility of a rescue operation, for example, without reliable information about the hostages' current circumstances.

Still, one can point to the importance of prolonging contact with the terrorists involved. The longer contact is maintained, the better the hostages' chances of survival. This is an extremely difficult process; to engage in negotiations with terrorists without succumbing to at least some of their demands is virtually a contradiction in terms. Terrorists may well be aware of this ploy and force a quick showdown by threatening to execute the hostages. Herein lies the possibility of a rescue operation. The difficult question for the government of Japan is whether it should be prepared to send its special rescue unit abroad. Even if a foreign local authority welcomes such an operation, there appear to be a number of legal and institutional hurdles to overcome.

—*The U.S.-Japanese Security Arrangement.* This scenario is different from the others in that it does not involve any impending armed conflict or violence. However, in terms of the magnitude of the stakes involved, it may be the most serious crisis for Japan. The rupture of the alliance between Japan and the United States would likely cause profound trauma in the populations of both countries. One may argue that if the alliance was terminated following cool-headed decisionmaking on both sides, perhaps there would be little to worry about. However, assuming that the two countries still shared basic values and a strategic interest in East Asia, it is inconceivable that cool-headed, rational decisionmaking in either country would produce the verdict that its national interest would be better served by terminating the alliance. As the scenario describes, uncontrollable xenophobia in both countries, whereby all of a sudden the unthinkable becomes thinkable, would be the most likely reason for ending the alliance. In the final analysis, what is always needed to avoid such an outcome are conscious and continuing efforts by the leaders of both countries to remind their people that they have much to gain in working together and too much to lose by ending the alliance.

—*Indian Ocean.* This scenario illustrates the risks that Japan would have to deal with single-handedly if the U.S.-Japanese alliance were to be terminated. In Japan, one tends to think of the alliance in terms of its role in deterring aggression in East Asia. However, the safety of tankers and other vessels that pass through the Indian Ocean is extremely important to Japan. In terms of ocean traffic, the Indian Ocean thus far has been tranquil, and no vessels bound for Japan have been interdicted there. The voyage becomes dangerous when vessels approach the coast of Southeast Asia, where piracy against relatively small vessels is quite common. Japan's tacit assumption is that in the event of hostile or disruptive actions by coastal states against Japanese ships in the Indian Ocean, the U.S. Seventh Fleet will intervene. It is also assumed that no coastal state around the Indian Ocean is likely to resort to any reckless action that would result in direct military confrontation with the United States. However, if an al Qaeda–type of fundamentalist group came to power in some coastal state, things could change. Theoretically, in the absence of U.S. naval protection, Japan would have to agonize over whether to expand its own naval capability to ensure the safety of vessels sailing to and from Japan. Here again, it is doubtful that the government could overcome the constitutional and political constraints that it has observed since the end of World War II.

In Closing

Toward the end of the twentieth century, the stability and effectiveness of the international order had been considerably enhanced by the deepening of a shared interest among nations in pursuing prosperity through the market mechanism; that in turn has prompted robust international economic interaction and widespread support for human rights and democratic forms of government. Gone are the days when centrally planned economies based on communist ideology were widely believed to be the better alternative. As the preceding chapters repeatedly point out, practically every country in East Asia has undergone a radical transformation, today attaching the highest national priority to economic development through the market mechanism and dynamic participation in the game of globalization. As a result, the regional security environment improved markedly compared with the period from the 1950s through the 1970s. During that time, the people's liberation agenda predominated, and the revolutionary axiom was that rural areas, that is, the poorer parts of the world, would come to engulf the urban areas, the rich capitalist countries. China's accession to the World Trade Organization in 1999 and its decision to allow owners of private enterprises—that is, capitalists—to join the Communist Party were the culmination of the truly fascinating changes that occurred in East Asia.

In other parts of the world, in particular the poorer parts, the quest for economic prosperity through globalization has not always been successful. Opponents of globalization continue to insist that the world as a whole will be worse off as a result of globalization. It is true that the market mechanism does not ensure the success of everyone; its basic function is to promote competition, and competition is bound to produce losers. Nor does the market mechanism ensure fairness in income distribution. Certainly the task of addressing poverty in that sense will remain an extremely important task on the international agenda.

The sharing of values has proceeded in tandem with the sharing of interests. In Europe, it followed the end of the cold war; in East Asia, it followed successful efforts to promote economic development, which produced a new middle class that became the driving force for democratization. Even so, the sharing of values remains an item of unfinished business in East Asia, where China and Vietnam still maintain political systems in which power is monopolized by the Communist Party. One wonders what to call such a system. Can it still be called communist when the Communist Party is likely to consist of a bunch of capitalists?

In other parts of the world, the effort to find common values often has not been easy. As can be seen in Iraq as well as Afghanistan, introducing democracy is an extremely difficult task. When a country is not equipped with the key prerequisites for democratization, such as the rule of law, and remains a captive of ethnic and tribal hatred, perhaps sharing values, in terms of democratization, is more difficult than sharing interests.

The security challenges that the international community has encountered in the aftermath of the cold war have come from players who have been utterly marginal in the international order and who share neither interests nor values with other nations. While traditional security threats have waned considerably, rogue states and al Qaeda–type terrorist groups have emerged as new deadly threats to international security. However, many European nations, notably France and Germany, did not share the United States' sense of urgency about the need for military action in Iraq in 2003. During the cold war, neither Germany nor France would have dared to take a position that could offend the United States to the degree that the Atlantic Alliance would be seriously weakened, simply because the Soviet Union was the primary adversary of them all. Free of any Soviet threat, Germany and France seemed to have concluded that they could afford to antagonize the United States by opposing the adoption of a new Security Council resolution that would have legitimized the use of force against Iraq.

When parties to an alliance cease to have a common enemy, the very foundation of the alliance is shaken. East European countries, notably

Poland, that believe that they still need the United States to counter the potential threat of Russia supported the U.S. position on Iraq. Japan's plight with regard to Iraq resembled that of the east Europeans. The argument in Japan on the eve of the war was that in view of the increasing threat of North Korea, Japan had to maintain a solid alliance with the United States and therefore had no option but to firmly support the U.S. position. That argument had strong support among the Japanese people.

Indeed, another alliance may be shaken as a result of no longer sharing an enemy. If South Korea comes to believe that North Korea no longer constitutes a threat to its security or that the presence of the U.S. military is hindering its reconciliation with North Korea, the foundation of the alliance between South Korea and the United States can be easily weakened. At the moment, the governments of both countries seem to be fully aware of that possibility and are making efforts to avert it.

In essence, in the post–cold war world the international order has become more civilized, stable, and effective because of the sharing of interests and values among nations, while the alliances among nations may undergo considerable realignment because they do not share enemies. Still, realignments of alliances are unlikely to disrupt the whole fabric of the international order, because of the predominance of shared interests and values. Now that the war in Iraq is over, obviously it would be in no one's interest to persist in undermining NATO and the United Nations, particularly to the point of their eventual demise.

In the current international setting, the basic orientation of Japanese foreign policy should be fairly obvious. Since, as discussed, neither Japan nor any other state can ensure its national security and well-being single-handedly, Japan must continue its quest to help construct and maintain an international as well as an Asian regional system of order. For that purpose, Japan must work with as many countries as possible to deepen and widen the sharing of interests and values among them, although finding common values may be a more difficult and sensitive undertaking. Meanwhile, in order to promote a better security environment, both global and regional, Japan should work to maintain an effective alliance with the United States; participate more actively in international endeavors to ensure peace and security, such as UN peacekeeping operations and multinational force operations pursuant to an authorizing Security Council resolution and within Japan's constitutional constraints; work with like-minded countries to seek the peaceful resolution of regional conflicts and help failed states to recover; and continue to provide substantial amounts of assistance in order to alleviate poverty, which can become a precursor of terrorism, throughout the world.

If Japan hopes to proceed along this course in a dynamic and imaginative manner, the country's first order of business is to recover its self-confidence. In that sense, Japan is at a crossroads. The rules of the game that led to remarkable economic growth in the post–World War II era—such as dependably consistent, consensus-oriented decisionmaking; lifetime employment; the convoy method of economic growth, which ensured the survival of the weakest members of various sectors; and the division of labor among the parliamentarians of the governing Liberal Democratic Party, bureaucrats, and business leaders, who together were referred to as the "iron triangle" (or, alternatively, as the "unholy trinity")—seem to have lost their effectiveness.

What the new rules might be remains unclear. Perhaps they will be based on more competition at the individual rather than the company level; perhaps the economic struggle will become more acute, with only the survival of the fittest ensured. If such Darwinian rules are introduced now, they will come at a time when the ratio of dependent elderly people to the young is on the rise. No wonder the Japanese are worried about the future. Under such circumstances, as pointed out in the opening chapter, resentment has become a significant facet of the national psyche. Obviously, it would be desirable for Japan to reverse its economic stagnation, which has lasted more than a decade—the result, perhaps, of the very rules that ensured the nation's earlier success.

It seems vital to rekindle Japan's dynamism and confidence in the future now, even though it will take some years to resolve the legacies of stagnation, notably nonperforming loans in the banking sector. If the nation continues its drift toward resentful nationalism, deeper entrenchment of its victim mentality, or a stronger proclivity to indulge in conspiracy theories to explain its misfortunes—all of which have been typical symptoms of trouble in many other countries in the long history of mankind—it is bound to have a disastrous impact on foreign policy. What, after all, is the point of Japan's pitying itself because it has become the victim of wicked foreigners' machinations? The two options that Japan exercised in the past, namely *sakoku* (the total closure of the state to the rest of the world) and the military domination of Asia, are not options in the twenty-first century.

If one looks back at the two defining periods in the modern history of Japan—the Meiji Restoration, when the country began to modernize, and the period immediately after its defeat in World War II—what stands out is that the nation's leaders were equipped with the vision, confidence, courage, and determination to chose the best course for Japan under extremely perilous and uncertain circumstances. Japan is in far better shape today, and the international situation is much safer and far more hospitable. As noted above, the basic orientation of the nation's foreign policy should be obvious and the steps Japan needs to take clear. What is needed now is to revive Japan's optimism and confidence in its destiny.

Bibliography

Arai, Toshiaki. *Henbou suru Chuugoku Gaikou—Keizai Juushi no Sekai Senryaku* (China's Changing Foreign Policy: Global Strategy in Pursuit of Economic Interest). Tokyo: Nichi-Chuu-Shuppan.

Cha, Victor. 1999. *Alignment despite Antagonism*. Stanford University Press.

Dower, John W. 1979. *Empire and Aftermath: Yoshida Shigeru and the Japanese Experience*. Harvard University, Council of East Asian Studies.

Green, Michael J. 2001. *Japan's Reluctant Realism: Foreign Policy Challenges in an Era of Uncertain Power*. New York: Council on Foreign Relations.

Hastings, Max. 1988. *The Korean War*. London: Pan Books.

Hosoya, Chihiro, ed. 2001. *Nihon to Amerika Partnership no 50 nen* (Japan and America: Fifty Years of Partnership). Tokyo: Japan Times.

Inoki, Takenori. 2000. *Keizai Seichou no Kajutu: 1955–1972* (Fruits of Economic Growth: 1955–1972). Vol. 7, *Nihon no Kindai* (A History of Modern Japan). Tokyo: Chuuou-Kouron-Sha.

Iokibe, Makoto. 2001. *Sensou, Senryou, Kouwa: 1941–1955* (War, Occupation, Peace: 1941–1955). Vol. 6, *Nihon no Kindai* (A History of Modern Japan). Tokyo: Chuuou-Kouron-Sha.

————. 1999. *Sengo Nihon Gaikoushi* (A History of Japan's Foreign Policy in the Postwar Era). Tokyo: Yuuhikaku.

Kitaoka, Shinichi. 1999. *Seitou kara Gunbu he: 1924–1941* (From Political Parties to Military Dominance): 1924–1941). Vol. 5, *Nihon no Kindai* (A History of Modern Japan). Tokyo: Chuuou-Kouron-Sha.

Kokubun, Ryousei, Kiichi Fujiwara, and Shinkou Hayashi, eds. *Global-ka sita Chuugoku wa dounaruka* (How Globalized China Is Likely to Change). Tokyo: Shinshokan.

Kouno, Masaharu. 1999. *Wahei Kousaku—Tai-Cambodia Gaikou no Shougen* (Peace Operation: Testimony of Diplomacy for Cambodia). Tokyo: Iwanami Shoten.

Lafeber, Walter. 1997. *The Clash: A History of U.S.-Japan Relations.* W.W. Norton & Company.

Mochizuki, Mike, ed. 1997. *Toward a True Alliance: Restructuring U.S.-Japan Security Relations.* Brookings.

Munakata, Naoko, ed. *Nichi-Chuu Kankei no Tenkanki* (The Turning Point of Relations between Japan and China). Tokyo: Toyoh-Keizai-Shinpoh-Sha.

Nakasone, Yasuhiro. 1999. *The Making of the New Japan.* Translated and annotated by Lesley Connors. Richmond, Surrey, U.K.: Curzon Press.

Oberdorfer, Don. 2001. *The Two Koreas: A Contemporary History.* Rev. ed. Basic Books.

Packard, George, III. 1978. *Protest in Tokyo: The Security Treaty Crisis of 1960.* Westport, Conn.: Greenwood Press.

Power, Samantha, and Graham Allison, eds. 2000. *Realizing Human Rights.* St. Martin's Press.

Sakamoto, Kazuya. 2000. *Nichi-Bei Doumei no Kizuna* (The Bond of the U.S.-Japan Alliance). Tokyo: Yuuhikaku.

Samejima, Keiji, ed. *Chuugoku no Seiki Nihon no Senryaku* (China's Century, Japan's Strategy). Tokyo: Nihon-Keizai-Shimbun.

Sotooka, Hidetoshi, Masaru Honda, and Toshiaki Miura. 2001. *Nichi-Bei Doumei Han-Seiki* (A Half-Century of the U.S.-Japan Alliance). Tokyo: Asahi-Shimbun.

Talbott, Strobe. 2002. *The Russia Hand.* Random House.

Togo, Fumihiko. 1989. *Nichi-Bei Gaikou 30 Nen—Nichi-Bei Anpo, Okinawa to Sonogo* (Thirty Years of Japan-U.S. Diplomacy: The Japan-U.S. Security Treaty, Okinawa and the Aftermath). Tokyo: Chuuou-Kouron-Sha.

Yabunaka, Mitoji. 1991. *Tai-Bei Keizai Koushou—Masatsu no Jitsuzou* (In Search of New Economic Relations between Japan and the United States: The View from the Negotiating Table). Tokyo: Simul Press.

Index

ADB. *See* Asian Development Bank
Afghanistan: democratization, 149; as
   a failed state, 135–37; human
   rights and humanitarian assistance,
   122, 138; Japan in, 138; Soviet
   invasion, 31; Taliban in, 51
Agreed Framework (1994; U.S.–North
   Korea), 88, 130
Albania, 136–37
Annan, Kofi, 137. *See also* United
   Nations
Antiterrorism Special Measures Law,
   42
APEC. *See* Asia Pacific Economic
   Cooperation forum
ASEAN. *See* Association of Southeast
   Asian Nations
ASEAN Regional Forum, 49
Asia: balance of power, 12; cold war
   in, 126; democratization, 105;
   domino theory, 29, 112, 113; East
   Asian economic crisis of 1997,
   122–25; economic issues, 105,
   110–11, 113–14, 119, 148, 149;
   human rights issues, 5, 13, 129;

Indonesia, 118–19; Japan and,
   4–5, 110–25; regional multilateral
   framework, 49–50; security issues,
   114–15; sharing of values, 149;
   strategic importance of Okinawa,
   43; trade issues, 19–20, 128–29;
   U.S. role in, 27, 45–46. *See also*
   individual countries
Asian Development Bank (ADB), 110
Asia Pacific Economic Cooperation
   forum (APEC), 6
Association of Southeast Asian
   Nations (ASEAN): EAEC and, 5–6;
   economic issues, 123; Japan and,
   111, 113, 115, 118, 125; Vietnam,
   Cambodia, and Laos, 112, 113
Aung San Suu Kyi, 121
Automobiles, 65, 66–67

Bali. *See* Indonesia
Balkans, 44, 130, 136–37
Bosnia, 130, 136, 137
Boxer Rebellion (1900; China), 105
Britain, 4–5, 140
Burma, 110. *See also* Myanmar

Bush, George W., 1–2, 52, 86, 92
Bush (George W.) administration, 88

Cambodia, 36, 112, 113–118,
    136–37, 138
Canada, 4
Carter, Jimmy, 13, 37, 79
Chiang Kai-shek, 97, 100
China, People's Republic of: Chinese
    view of the world, 106–07; Com-
    munist Party, 104, 106, 109;
    Cultural Revolution, 97, 111;
    democratization, 101, 104–05,
    133; Falun Gong, 105; Gang of
    Four, 98; Great Leap Forward, 97;
    historical background, 96–99, 103;
    military issues, 101–02, 107–09;
    political issues, 104–06, 109;
    Tiananmen Square massacre, 14,
    95, 99, 104, 115, 126; trade issues,
    19, 68, 99–100, 102–03, 124;
    WTO and, 99, 148; worst-case sce-
    narios, 142–44. *See also* Taiwan
    and Taiwan Straits
China, People's Republic of—eco-
    nomic issues: under Deng Xiaop-
    ing, 98–100; economic develop-
    ment and growth, 2, 17, 107, 111,
    133; Japan and, 101–03, 104–06,
    109, 110; "Reform and Opening,"
    84; trade, 99, 123, 148
China, People's Republic of—foreign
    policy: East Asian Economic Cau-
    cus and, 6; foreign direct invest-
    ment, 123; Japan and, 12, 14, 17,
    29, 75, 95–109, 111; Khmer
    Rouge, 115; Korea and, 46, 47,
    74, 77–78, 93; Myanmar and, 121;
    Peace and Friendship Treaty, 98;
    Soviet Union and, 29–30; U.S. and,
    29, 45, 97, 106, 108; Vietnam and,
    112–13
Churchill, Winston, 53
Clinton, Bill, 66
Clinton (Bill) administration, 56,
    63–64, 69, 86, 134

Cold war: adversarial relations, 22;
    Cambodia, 113, 114; containment
    policies during, 45; deterrence dur-
    ing, 51, 87; end of, 126–27, 134,
    136; European countries and, 33,
    127–31, 149; Japan and, 7, 9,
    12–13, 24, 34, 47–48, 111–12,
    126, 132–33, 134; Korea and, 76,
    77; post–cold war period, 38–41,
    44, 126, 127–29, 150; Reagan,
    Ronald and, 13, 31, 59–60;
    renewal of, 31; Soviet Union and,
    12, 13, 127; United Nations and,
    136; United States and, 12, 13, 23,
    28, 32, 33, 38
Committee to Change the Foreign
    Ministry, 3
Communism and communists: in
    China, 148, 149; in Europe, 127;
    in Iraq, 149; Japanese views of,
    12–13, 24, 25, 126; nationalism
    and, 133; victory in Indochina, 30;
    in Vietnam, 149
Comprehensive Test Ban Treaty, 53
Computers. *See* Technology
Conservatives and conservatism. *See*
    Political issues—Japan
Constitution (Japan). *See* Japan;
    Japanese Self-Defense Force

Democracy and democratization: in
    Asia, 13, 105; in China, 104–06,
    146; in Europe, 128; in Indonesia,
    119; in Japan, 141; Japanese
    views of, 11, 12–13; need for,
    140–41; in post-conflict countries,
    141, 149; in Russia, 133, 134,
    140–41; in Taiwan, 105, 109,
    146
Democratic People's Republic of
    Korea (DPRK). *See* Korea
Deng Xiaoping, 84, 96, 98–99, 100,
    104
Deterrence. *See* Military issues
DPRK (Democratic People's Republic
    of Korea). *See* Korea

EAEC. *See* East Asian Economic Caucus

East Asian Economic Caucus (EAEC), 5–6

East Timor, 120, 129, 136–37

Economic issues: in Asia, 13, 45; bubble economy, 60; cold war and post–cold war eras, 127–28; dispute resolution, 69–70; East Asian economic crisis of 1997, 122–25; in Europe, 128; GATT and, 19; globalization, 148–49; in Korea, 77, 78; Miyazawa plan, 123; most-favored nations, 65, 67–68; in the U.S., 56, 60, 61–62, 63, 68, 70–71

Economic issues—Japan: Bretton Woods system, 1, 24; China and, 97; development, ix, 4, 55–56, 151; difficulties of, 3, 68, 72, 151; dispute resolution, 69–70; East Asian economic crisis of 1997, 122–25; economic targets, 65–66, 69, 71; Europe and, 130–31; foreign direct investment, 123, 124; framework talks, 64–65, 66, 71–72; human rights and sanctions, 13–14; Ikeda, Hayato and, 28; internationalism, 15–16; Korean War, 24; Plaza Accord, 113, 123; post–World War II, 18–19; promotion of economic development, 142; Russia and, 133; security factors, 59–60; trade, 19–20, 56–72, 110, 124–25, 128; U.S. and, 16, 55–72; Vietnam and, 118; vulnerabilities, 18–21, 30. *See also* Official Development Assistance program; Oil

Economist, 53

EU. *See* European Union

Europe: anti-immigration views, 3; antiterrorism, 41; balance of power, 12; cold war period, 127, 129; cultural issues, 128; Indonesia, 120; Iraq war, 129–30, 149–50; Japan and, 127–31; political issues, 129–30; United States and, 33, 52–53, 71; wars and invasions, 9, 19

European Common Market, 19

European Union (EU): development of, 128, 129; EAEC and, 6; horizontal division of labor, 124; Japan and, 130; Korean nuclear development, 130; Myanmar and, 121; trade issues, 63, 67–68, 71

Fair Trade Commission, 62

Foreign Ministry, 3. *See also* Foreign policy—Japan

Foreign policy, 12

Foreign policy—Japan: agenda of, viii, 1–2, 135–36, 150–52; cold war era, 12–13, 111–12, 127–31; Europe and, 130; Fukuda Doctrine, 112; imperialist expansion, 18; international issues, 12, 20; Iraq war, 150; Japan's Asian identity, 4–6; post–Vietnam War, 115–16; post–World War II, 4–11, 14–15, 20, 151–52; public opinion and demands, 3, 6; security issues, 6–11; Treaty of Security and Mutual Cooperation between Japan and the United States of America (1960), 26, 27, 28–33, 144–45, 147–48; U.S.-Japan security treaty, 8, 9, 16–17, 23–28, 38–41, 144–45, 147–48. *See also* International issues; Official Development Assistance program; Political issues—Japan; Security arrangements; World War II; individual countries

France, 6, 116, 140, 149

Fukuda Doctrine, 112

Futenma Air Station, 44

G-6 countries, 4, 20

G-7 countries, 32, 64, 99

G-8 countries, 129

GATT. *See* General Agreement on Tariffs and Trade
Gaullism, 33, 48–49
General Agreement on Tariffs and Trade (GATT), 19, 60, 65, 66, 72, 124
Germany, 22–23, 126, 127, 149
Glasnost, 140–41
Globalization. *See* International issues
Gorbachev, Mikhail, 140–41
Greece, 127

Haiti, 136–37
Hashimoto, Ryutaro, 67
Hatoyama, Ichiro, 33, 132
Heng Samrin, 113
Hideyoshi, Toyotomi, 74
Higuchi Committee, 49
Hitler, Adolf, 88
Hong Kong, 58, 109, 113
Hosokawa, Morihiro, 66
Human rights: in Afghanistan, 122; in Bosnia, 137; in China, 99; European Union and, 129; humanitarian assistance and, 122; in Indonesia and East Timor, 120; in Japanese foreign policy, 13; Japanese views of, 5, 99; in North Korea, 87; in Rwanda, 137; United Nations and, 137; use of force, 142
Hun Sen, 113, 115–16, 117
Hussein, Saddam, 52, 87, 140. *See also* Iraq; Persian Gulf War

IAEA. *See* International Atomic Energy Agency
Idealism. *See* Political issues—Japan
Ikeda, Hayato, 28
India, 12, 44, 145
Indian Ocean, 145, 147–48
Indochina, 30, 111, 112, 114–15
Indonesia: ASEAN and, 116; Bali terrorist attack, 51; democratization, 105, 119, 121; economic issues, 111, 113, 119, 120, 123; Japan

and, 120; political crises, 44, 118–21; as a source of oil, 18; United Nations, 120; World War II reparations, 110; worst-case scenario, 144, 146–47
International Atomic Energy Agency (IAEA), 79
International Criminal Court, 53
International issues: abduction of foreign nationals, 81; Cambodia, 113–18; economic factors, 114, 148; enforcement of human rights, 142; globalization, 17, 53–54, 100, 107–08, 148–49; Indonesia, 120; maintenance of international order and security, 12, 34, 53, 114, 148; nationalism, 119; post–cold war period, 44; security, 149; sharing of interests and values, ix, 149, 150; trade, 58–59; uncertainty in, 1; U.S. economy and, 68. *See also* Foreign policy; Terrorism and antiterrorism
Internet, 100
Iran, 31
Iraq: Operation Desert Fox bombing campaign (1998), 51–52; democratization, 149; as a failed state, 136; reconstruction of, 23, 140; United Nations and, 129–30; U.S. policies, 87, 88. *See also* Persian Gulf war
Islamic revolution and fundamentalism, 3, 31, 51, 144, 145
Israel, viii, 51–52
Italy, 127

Japan: Asian identity, 4–5, 32; constitution, 6, 7, 27, 28, 33, 35, 39; cultural issues, 128; crises, viii–ix; democratization, 141; generational turnover, 2; historical background, 73–77; human rights in, 5; *keiretsu*, 61; Korea and, 46–47; military, 6–7; national identity, 4–5; Northern Territory, 131–32, 133; post–cold war period, 38–41,

126, 128; post–World War II, 23, 128, 140, 151–52; public opinion in, 3, 6, 9–10, 16–17; regional multilateral framework, 49–50; saving failed states, 141–42; U.S. antiterrorism campaign, 1–2; U.S. views of, 56; worst-case scenarios, 142–45. *See also* Economic issues—Japan; Foreign policy—Japan; Political issues—Japan

Japanese Self-Defense Force (JSDF): antiterrorism measures, 41–42; cold war issues, 12, 31; constitutional issues, 7–8, 33, 35, 39, 41; creation of, 27, 33; defense capabilities, 32; legitimacy of, viii; peacekeeping operations, 10, 35–37; public opinion of, 9–10; role and mission, 10, 33–38, 39–41, 83, 138, 141b; United Nations multinational force, 137–38

Japan–United States Joint Declaration on Security, 38

Jiang Zemin, 100

Johnson, Chalmers, 56

Joint Declaration of 1956 (Japan-Russia), 133

Joint Statement of Prime Minister Eisaku Sato and President Richard Nixon (1969), 29

JSDF. *See* Japanese Self-Defense Force

Kagan, Robert, 130

Kanemaru, Shin, 82

Kantor, Michael, 67

Kashmir, 44

KEDO. *See* Korean Peninsula Energy Development Organization

Khmer Rouge, 112, 113, 115, 116, 117

Khomeini, Ayatollah, 31

Kim Dae Jung: Japan and, 77, 93; nuclear-arming of North Korea, 92; sunshine policy, 46, 80, 84, 85

Kim Il Sung, 75, 78

Kim Jong Il, 78, 80, 81, 82, 86

Kishi, Shinsuke, 26, 28, 32

Kissinger, Henry, 12, 29

KMT. *See* Kuomintang party

Kohl, Helmut, 127

Koizumi, Junichiro, 8, 81, 82, 103

Konoe, Fumimaro, 5

Korea: 1960s, 29; abduction of Japanese citizens, 2, 73, 81–82, 83, 90; anti-Americanism, 90–91; China and, 74, 97; democratization, 105; division and unification, 46–47, 73, 75–76, 77–78, 79, 80, 90–91, 97, 150; East Asian Economic Caucus and, 6; economic issues, 83, 84, 88–89, 91, 92, 123; European Union and, 130; foreign relations, 77–78, 83–84; historical background, 74–77; humanitarian aid to, 82–83, 85, 89, 121; Japan and, 73–74, 76–77, 79–82, 86–87, 89–90, 93–94, 111, 150; military issues, 84–85; North-South Summit, 80; post–cold war period, 39, 41, 45; Russia and, 74, 134; sunshine policy of the South, 46, 80, 84, 85; trade issues, 58, 124; United Nations and, 37, 79, 88–89; U.S. and, 24, 46–47, 74, 76, 79–80, 85, 86, 88, 90; worst-case scenario, 142–43, 145–46

Korea—nuclear development of the North: causes and effects of, 2, 37, 44, 46, 73, 78, 83–84, 89; China and, 93; inspections, 79; international consultation and cooperation, 79–80; Japan and, 86, 90, 91–92, 130; historical background, 78–80; light-water reactor, 79, 130; missile launch over Japan, 41, 79, 83; options for possible solutions, 87–94; Republic of Korea (South Korea) and, 85, 90, 92; Russia and, 93; U.S. and, 86, 87, 88–89, 90, 91–93; war and, 88, 92

Korean Peninsula Energy Development Organization (KEDO), 37, 79, 130
Korean War (1950–53), 23, 24, 25, 75–76
Kosovo, 15, 53, 129, 137, 142
Kuomintang party (KMT; Taiwan), 100
Kuwait, 34, 35
Kyoto Protocol, 53

Laos, 112, 115, 118
Lee Hoi Chang, 85
Liberal Democratic Party (LDP), 2, 8, 28–29, 97
Liberal Party, 35

MacArthur, Douglas, 25
Mahathir bin Mohamad, 5–6
Malaysia, 113, 123
Manchuria, 131
Maritime Safety Agency (Japan), 37
Media, 69, 119
Meiji Restoration (1868), 4, 75, 131, 151–52
Middle East, 20, 30, 45, 78
Militarism. *See* Political issues—Japan
Military issues: abduction of foreign nationals, 81–82; alliances, 149–50; ballistic missiles, 127; Bush preemptive strike doctrine, 1–2, 87, 88; casus belli, 81, 82; democracy and, 11; deterrence, 9–10, 50, 51–52, 78; future threats, 38; mutually assured destruction, 84–85, 86, 87; rogue states, 87; unarmed neutrality, 25, 47–48; U.S. military bases, 17, 26, 27, 43–44, 45, 50. *See also* individual countries
Military issues—Japan: antiterrorism, 41–42, 50–54; comprehensive and regional security, 30, 28–33, 38–41, 44–50; constitution and, 7–8, 33, 35, 39, 41; defense spend-

ing, 30; deterrence, 27, 32, 34; independently oriented defense, 32–33; peacekeeping operations, 9, 10; public opinion, 9–10; unarmed neutrality, 25–26, 32, 47–48; use of nuclear weapons, 27. *See also* Japanese Self-Defense Force; Okinawa; Treaty of Security and Mutual Cooperation between Japan and the United States of America; U.S.-Japan security treaty and arrangements
Ministerial Conference for Agricultural Development (1966), 110
Mongolia and Mongolians, 74
Munich Agreement, 88
Murayama, Tomiichi, 14
Muslims. *See* Islamic revolution and fundamentalism
Myanmar, 121–22, 129. *See also* Burma

Nakae, Chomin, 4
Nakasone, Yasuhiro, 11, 31–32, 60, 127
Nationalism. *See* Political issues—Japan
National League for Democracy (NLD; Myanmar), 121, 122
NATO. *See* North Atlantic Treaty Organization
New Age Economic Partnership (2002; Japan-Singapore), 1124
Nixon, Richard M., 29
NLD. *See* National League for Democracy
North Atlantic Treaty Organization (NATO), 33, 50, 142
Nye, Joseph S., Jr., 53

Oberdofer, Don, 78
Obuchi, Keizo, 93–94
ODA. *See* Official Development Assistance program
Office of the United States Trade Representative, 67

Official Development Assistance program (ODA): ASEAN and, 123–24; China and, 101–02; Indonesia and, 111, 120; Myanmar and, 121; political issues, 111–12, 122, 138; Vietnam and, 113, 118

Ohira, Masayoshi, 31

Oil: embargoes, crises, and shortages, 20, 30; Indonesia as supplier of, 18; Japanese use of, 18, 20–21, 31; Middle East as supplier of, 20; U.S. as supplier of, 18, 20

Okinawa, 9, 29, 42–44, 50, 144

Olympic Games (1980, 1988, 2008), 31, 77, 106

Omnibus Trade and Competitiveness Act (1988), 60

Operation Desert Fox (1998), 51–52

Ozawa, Ichiro, 35

Pacifism and pacifists. *See* Political issues—Japan

Pakistan, 44, 145

Paris Peace Conference (1989), 116, 117

Park Chung Hee, 76

Peace and Friendship Treaty (Japan-China), 98

People's Liberation Army (PLA), 108. *See also* China, People's Republic of

People's Republic of China (PRC). *See* China, People's Republic of

Perestroika, 140–41

Perry, Matthew, 131

Perry report (1999), 78, 79–80, 87

Persian Gulf war (1991), 33–38

Philippines, 110, 113–14, 118

PLA. *See* People's Liberation Army

Plaza Accord (1985), 113, 123

Poland, 149–50

Political issues: decisionmaking, 2–3; diplomacy, 3; in the European Union, 128–29; U.S.-Japanese trade, 56; U.S. military bases, 44

Political issues—Japan: apologists and nonapologists, 14–15, 103; Asian identity, 4–5, 32; China, 95; comprehensive security, 30–31; conservatives, 33; decisionmaking, 2, 142; Gaullism, 48–49; idealists and realists, 6–14, 24, 29, 30, 33, 34, 39, 77, 111, 120, 121–22, 138; Indonesia, 120; Korea, 75–77; Myanmar, 121–22; nationalism and internationalism, 15–18, 115, 133, 151; pacifists and realists, 6–11, 24, 25–26, 27, 29, 30, 31, 32, 33, 34, 35–36, 39, 41, 42, 49, 52, 77, 86–87, 111–12, 138; Persian Gulf war, 34; public opinion and views, 10–11, 32, 42, 52–53, 151–52; security and militarism, 6–10, 25–26, 32; trade, 57, 69–71; United Nations, 24, 137–38, 139–0. *See also* Liberal Democratic Party; Treaty of Security and Mutual Cooperation between Japan and the United States of America; U.S.-Japan security treaty and arrangements

PRC (People's Republic of China). *See* China, People's Republic of

Putin, Vladimir, 134

Ranariddh (Prince; Cambodia), 116

Reagan, Ronald, 13, 31–32, 59–60, 127

Reagan (Ronald) administration, 31

Realists and Realism. *See* Political issues—Japan

Republic of Korea (ROK). *See* Korea

Roh Moo Hyun, 80, 85, 92

ROK (Republic of Korea). *See* Korea

Russia: Gorbachev, Mikhail, 140–41; imperial Russia, 75; Japan and, 12; Northern Territory, 126, 131–34; North Korean nuclear development, 74, 93; as a potential threat, 149–50. *See also* Soviet Union

Russo-Japanese War (1904–05), 75, 131

Rwanda, 136–37

Ryukyu Islands, 43

SACO. *See* Special Action Committee on Okinawa

San Francisco Peace Treaty, 77, 98, 132

Sato, Eisaku, 29

Section 301, 60

Security and security arrangements. *See* Military issues; Terrorism and antiterrorism; Treaty of Security and Mutual Cooperation between Japan and the United States of America; United Nations; U.S.-Japan security treaty and arrangements

Self-Defense Force. *See* Japanese Self-Defense Force

Semiconductors. *See* Technology

September 11, 2001, 41, 45, 51, 86, 134. *See also* Terrorism and antiterrorism

Shaping Our Common Future: An Action Plan for EU-Japan Cooperation, 131

Siberia, 132, 133

Sihanouk (Prince; Cambodia), 116, 117

Singapore, 5, 6, 113, 123, 124–25

Sino-Japanese War (1894), 75

Special Action Committee on Okinawa (SACO), 43–44

Somalia, 136–37

Soviet Union: 1980 Olympic Games, 31; China and, 29–30; cold war issues, 12, 13, 127; disintegration of, 105, 108; Japan and, 38, 131–33; Korea and, 75, 77–78, 80; Reagan, Ronald and, 59–60; United States and, 33; Vietnam and, 31, 112, 113, 115. *See also* Cold war

SII. *See* Structural Impediment Initiative

SLORC. *See* State Law and Order Restoration Council

State Law and Order Restoration Council (SLORC; Myanmar), 121, 122

Structural Impediment Initiative (SII), 56, 61–62, 70

Suharto, 111, 119

Sukarno, 111

Summit of the Industrial Democracies (G-6; 1975), 20

Super 301 clause, 60–61, 64, 66, 68, 69, 70–71

Suzuki, Zenko, 31

Switzerland, 25

Taiwan and Taiwan Strait: China and, 95–96, 100, 108; democratization, 105, 109; economic issues, 113, 123; Japan and, 44, 47, 97–98, 103–04, 108–09; Okinawa and, 29; trade issues, 58; worst-case scenario, 143–44, 146

Talbott, Strobe, 134

Taliban. *See* Afghanistan

Tanaka, Kakuei, 57, 97

Techonology, 62, 67, 71, 100

Terrorism and antiterrorism: Bush preemptive strike doctrine, 1–2, 87, 88; international security, 149; international views of, 45; Japan-Russia cooperation, 134; use of JSDF, 8, 36, 41–42; U.S. views of, 86; war on terrorism, 50–54; worst case scenario, 144, 146–47

Thailand, 105, 112, 113, 116, 123

Thatcher, Margaret, 127

Trade. *See* Economic issues

Trade Act of 1974, 60

Treaty of Security and Mutual Cooperation between Japan and the United States of America (1960), 26, 27, 28–33, 144–45

UN. *See* United Nations
United Kingdom. *See* Britain
United Nations (UN): charter of, 7,
    24, 48; international conferences,
    137; Iraq war, 129–30, 149–150;
    Japan and, 6–7, 23–24, 135–40;
    multinational force, 35, 48, 136,
    137–38; North Korea, 37, 79,
    88–89; peacekeeping, 35, 135–38,
    139; Persian Gulf war, 35; Security
    Council, 136, 137, 138–40;
    weapons of mass destruction, 52.
    See also individual countries
United States (U.S.): antiterrorism
    campaign, 1–2; cold war period,
    129; economic and trade policy,
    18–19, 55–72, 110–11, 123;
    Japanese resentment toward, 4–5,
    16–17; military bases, 17, 26,
    27, 43–44, 45, 46–47, 50; power
    of, 53–54; role of the military,
    11; as supplier of oil, 18; trade
    issues, 56; worst-case scenarios,
    142–45
United States—foreign policy, 17,
    52–53: East Asian Economic Cau-
    cus, 6; Iran hostage crisis, 31;
    Japan and, 6, 7, 16, 22–23, 31;
    Persian Gulf war, 34. *See also*
    Treaty of Security and Mutual
    Cooperation between Japan and
    the United States of America; indi-
    vidual countries
United States-Japan security treaty
    and arrangements: background of,
    16–17, 23–28; political issues, 8, 9,
    16–17, 24–26; redefinition of,

38–41; worst-case scenarios,
    144–45, 147. *See also* Treaty of
    Security and Mutual Cooperation
    between Japan and the United
    States of America

Vietnam, 31, 110, 112–13, 115–16,
    118
Vietnam War (1960s), 29, 30, 111,
    112–13

World Bank, 114
World Cup (soccer, 2002), 16, 94
World Trade Organization (WTO):
    China and, 99, 105, 148; dispute
    settlement, 60, 68, 71–72; Japan
    and, 66, 71–72, 124, 130–31; U.S.
    and, 66, 68, 71–72
World War I, 9, 22, 137
World War II: effects of, 4, 10–11,
    18–19; kamikaze, 74; Japan and,
    5, 14, 16, 75; Korea and, 75; Oki-
    nawa, 43; reparations, 110; war
    dead, 137
WTO. *See* World Trade Organization

Yasukuni Shrine, 15, 103
Yomiuri (newspaper), 11
Yom Kippur War (1973), 20, 30
Yoshida Doctrine, 9
Yoshida, Shigeru: China and, 19, 97;
    economic views, 7, 18; Japanese
    Self-Defense Force, 27, 33; Korean
    War, 24; U.S.-Japan security treaty,
    25, 26, 27, 132; Yoshida Doctrine,
    9
Yugoslavia, 15, 108

About the Author

Yutaka Kawashima served as Japan's vice
minister of foreign affairs from 1999 to 2001
and as ambassador to Israel from 1997 to
1999. After his retirement he did research as a
distinguished visiting fellow at the Brookings
Institution's Center for Northeast Asian Policy
Studies and taught at the John F. Kennedy
School of Government, Harvard University.
He has served in Asia, Europe, and the United
States and is widely respected in international
policy circles.